IRELAND

DUMONT GUIDE
IRELAND

by
WOLFGANG ZIEGLER
translated by
RUSSELL STOCKMAN

STEWART, TABORI & CHANG
PUBLISHERS, NEW YORK

FRONT COVER:
Rock of Cashel, Tipperary (© John Bryson/The Image Bank)
BACK COVER, TOP:
Ballingeary, Cork (© Blaine Harrington)
BACK COVER, BOTTOM:
Connemera, Galway (© D'Lynn Waldron/The Image Bank)
BACK FLAP:
Kerry (© Dr. E. R. Degginger)
INSIDE BACK FLAP:
Adaptation of map of Dublin from *The Irish Answer* by Tony Gray, 1966
(Reprinted by permission of Little Brown and Company)
PAGES 2—3:
A 19th-century view of Dublin, steel engraving by Rouargue
FRONTISPIECE:
Map of Ireland from William Petty's *Hiberniae delineato* (1865)

Library of Congress Cataloging in Publication Data
Ziegler, Wolfgang, 1950–
DuMont guide to Ireland.
Translation of: Irland.
Bibliography: p.
Includes index.
1. Ireland—Description and travel—1981– Guidebooks.
I. Title.
DA980.Z5313   1984   914.15'04824   83-18167
ISBN 0-941434-44-3

Distributed in the United States by
Workman Publishing Co., Inc., 1 West 39th Street
New York, N.Y. 10018.
Printed in Spain.

CONTENTS

PRACTICAL TRAVEL SUGGESTIONS

THE
ART, CULTURE
AND
HISTORY OF IRELAND

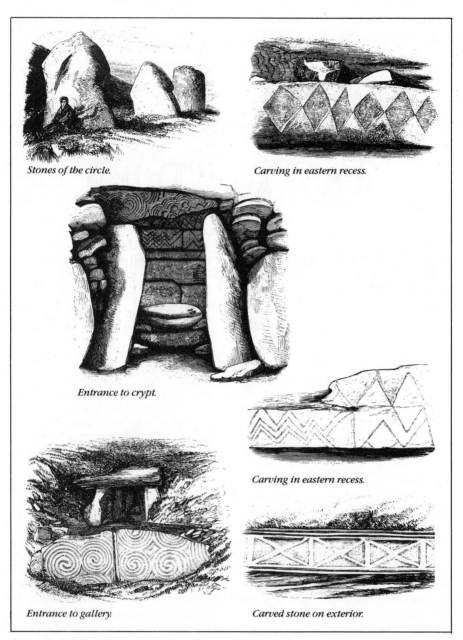

Stones of the circle.

Carving in eastern recess.

Entrance to crypt.

Carving in eastern recess.

Entrance to gallery.

Carved stone on exterior.

Remains of a passage grave at Newgrange, Meath.

THE STONE AGE

Archeological excavation reveals that Ireland was first visited by humans in the Mesolithic period, roughly 6000 B.C. These early arrivals were hunters and fishermen from Scotland who landed on the north coast and in time penetrated to the south and west, as far as the present-day cities of Newry and Dublin. Cultivation of the land did not take place until the next wave of immigrants came 3,000 years later. These were farmers who had stone tools and could till the land. From that era until the present, there has been a continual effort to work the land. As a result, Ireland now has fewer forests than any other country in Europe; they constitute only 2 percent of its land surface.

These early farmers lived in huts built of stones that were piled on top of one another without mortar. Roofs were made of straw or moss, later of stone. Remains of the walls of these huts can be found, especially in the vicinity of Lough Gur (Limerick).

Megalithic Tombs

More imposing than the houses of the living were the tombs they built. These provide an accurate picture of the technical skills of the people of that time. Megalithic tombs are so named because of the massive stone blocks of which they are constructed; the term encompasses a variety of grave sites.

Passage Graves

The simplest and oldest form is the passage grave (illus. 3, page 34), from the Neolithic period, with one or more chambers. A corridor formed by large, squared, vertical stones decorated with simple ornaments and covered with earth leads to a central burial chamber. Remains of funeral objects found in these chambers can be dated by the radiocarbon method to between 3000 and 2500 B.C. In more recent examples, such as the Boyne Valley tombs at Newgrange (illus. 4–6, page 35) and Dowth, the central chamber is surrounded by a number of smaller chambers, usually three, giving the tomb a cross-shaped ground plan. Sacrificial stones hollowed out to form basins have been discovered in these smaller chambers, suggesting a well-developed cult of the dead and repeated use of the tomb. The numerous ornaments are an interesting testimony to a primitive belief in the hereafter. Double spirals, triangles, and zigzag lines common to a number of cultures decorate the chambers and the passageway, as does the ever-present symbol of the sun.

Because of its puzzling similarity to tombs in Portugal, the grave at Fourknocks Hill, northwest of Haul, suggests that its builders may have belonged to a minor wave of immigration from the Iberian Peninsula. The tombs of the Boyne Valley in central Ireland, however, are closely related to British examples. Other passage tombs can be found throughout the entire region of Celtic influence, and in northern Germany, the Netherlands, France, and Spain. Passage tombs were built in Ireland until roughly 2000 B.C.—much later than on the Continent, where dolmens replaced them after about 2500 B.C.

Dolmens

The term *dolmen* derives from the Breton word meaning "stone table." Also called portal tomb, the dolmen consists of a chamber formed by several vertical bearing stones, generally five or six, that support a huge capstone. The bearing stones often become smaller toward the "portal," so that the roofing stone slopes upward to form the entrance; the contact surface between the stones was often astonishingly small. In many tombs some of the bearing stones are sunk into the ground, and the large roof, as at Browne's Hill (illus. 2, page 34), lies level with the ground. The construction of dolmens was clearly a tedious undertaking. First, the bearing stones were set up, after which a hill of earth was presumably built around them. The roof slab was then dragged up this artificial hill, and finally the earth was dug away again, leaving a freestanding tomb chamber.

Dolmens can be found not only throughout Europe but in northern Israel and Jordan as well. Through chemical analysis of charcoal traces, they can be dated to the Copper Age (2000 B.C.–c. 1750 B.C.). The largest dolmens in Ireland are those at Browne's Hill (Carlow), Proleek (Louth), and Knockeen (Waterford).

Seeing these colossal structures, one cannot help but admire the skill and technical

Dolmen at Tawnatruffaun, Sligo.

accomplishment of their builders. One can almost sense here something of the mysterious and awesome power that must have surrounded the sacrificial ceremonies and meditative rites.

Gallery Graves

Gallery graves are a variant of the passage graves, described above, in which there is no division between passage and chamber. The large chamber of squared stones extends underneath a generally elongated burial mound. Countless variations on this tomb form may be found in Catalonia. A wave of immigration from France (3000 B.C.) may have brought the practice of building gallery tombs to Ireland.

Passage grave at Hazelwood, Sligo.

THE BRONZE AGE

Its gold, copper, and bronze may well have made Ireland one of the largest producers of metals in the world during the Bronze Age (c. 1750 B.C.–500 B.C.). The crescent-shaped gold disks that can now be admired at the National Museum in Dublin were highly sought after objects of trade. The island's location on sea routes between the Mediterranean and the North and Baltic seas allowed it to become involved in world commerce, and it was probably at this time that Ireland first came into closer contact with other countries, especially Britain.

Stone circles, or *cromlechs* (a Welsh word meaning "curved flat stones"), are relics of this epoch, and several beautiful examples are preserved in Ireland—for example, those at Grange and on Lough Gur, as well as the Piper's Stones and the stone circles at Beltany in the north. Except for a few examples in Brittany, stone circles are found exclusively in the British Isles, where their form varies from place to place. Typical of the Irish cromlech is a recumbent stone with the two tallest vertical stones placed diametrically opposite it. In England, on the contrary, the two largest stones flank the horizontal one. Stone circles were the setting for cult sacrifices and celebrations; in some of them—for example, at Drombeg (Cork) (illus. 8, page 36)—funerary objects, such as characteristic stoneware jugs, have been excavated.

Certain *menhirs* (a Breton word meaning "long stones") also date from the Bronze Age. Menhirs served as tombstones and as boundary stones and markers. They may be regarded as the predecessors of Christian high crosses.

THE IRON AGE

It is not entirely clear when the first Celtic immigration to Ireland took place. However, the island was completely populated by Celts by the end of the fifth century B.C. The Celtic peoples brought a new social order that would stamp the life of Ireland for almost a thousand years. A knowledge of this system is necessary in order to understand Irish culture. Until the beginning of the Christian era, there was no actual writing and therefore no recorded history; legends and countless sagas are our only sources for study.

The island was divided into various kingdoms whose rulers, in contrast to the majority of the population, which was nomadic, maintained fixed and fortified residences. The characteristic social unit was the *deirbhfine*, or "kin-group," an extended family. Local groups of clans, called *tuatha*, were ruled by petty kings (*rí*) who sometimes in turn paid tribute to a provincial king (*rí ruirech*). Monarchs, credited with magical powers, were responsible for the success or failure of wars, crops, and even hunting and fishing expeditions.

These rulers also attracted "wise men" of the privileged class to their courts, the centers of cultural life. The *aes dána* constituted this high class. Headed by the Druids, priests, and magicians, it was also made up of doctors, historians, legal scholars, goldsmiths, poets, and bards. As in later times, each ruler sought to gather about himself as many as possible of these men, although they were also permitted to travel freely throughout the country. Members of the *aes dána* could cross the borders between kingdoms without fear, but it was expressly forbidden for members of the warrior caste and the common people to do so. The Ulaidh, who ruled the northern kingdom from Eamhain Macha, stationed guards at their borders to provide a princely welcome to members of the *aes dána*. When the country became more unsettled as a result of the many tribal feuds, the kings chose from among themselves a high king (*ard rí*) whose job it was to maintain peace by means of the *fianna*, his powerful troops.

Construction of tombs became less important during the Iron Age. In fact, we know very little about the burial customs of this epoch. Characteristic of the Iron Age are its fortifications, the work of its goldsmiths, and the Ogham stones.

Iron Age Fortifications

Ring Forts

The earliest ring forts were built in the Bronze Age, but they continued to be built into the early Christian period. Ring forts were fortified farmsteads, mud-daubed timber and wattle huts enclosed by a rampart. Raths had an earth rampart; cashels were enclosed by stone walls.

Many ring forts had *souterrains*, underground passageways of stone that were connected to the dwellings and were used for storage and refuge.

Hill Forts

More permanent fortifications generally crowned the summits of hills, as at Grianán of Aileach (Donegal), and were fortified by one or more encircling walls. Trenches and

Ballykinvarga Stone Fort, a mortarless ring fort near Kilfenora, Clare.

outworks often served to strengthen the circular or oval site further—sometimes, as at Tara (Meath), constructed around a Bronze Age tomb. This method of construction came to the island with La Tène culture (the Celtic culture of the Continent), and it survived in Ireland much longer than in the rest of Europe. Many hill forts contained round or square wooden huts; their foundations were made of piles of stones in the northern regions, where wood was scarce. These forts generally served military functions, but some of them, like Tara, were permanent royal residences that offered refuge to the people living in clusters of huts outside them. Hill forts were constructed as late as our own century to protect cattle.

Well-preserved examples of hill forts are Grianán of Aileach (illus. 64 and 65, page 124), Dún Ailinne (Kildare), Staigue (Kerry) (illus. 67, page 125), and Rathcoran, on Baltinglass Hill (Wicklow).

Promontory Forts

To create a promontory fort, a tongue of land reaching far out into the sea was built up so that walls and trenches provided protection on the land side, while steep cliffs made conquest from the sea virtually impossible. Impressive promontory forts can be seen at Dunbeg (Kerry), Caherconree (Kerry), and Dún Aengus (illus. 66, page 125), on Inishmore, the largest of the Aran Islands.

Crannógs

These fortifications are less common than ring forts because constructing them was difficult and time-consuming. Crannógs are artificial islands or dwelling platforms, often so small that there is room for only a single hut. The platforms were built out of layers of turf, wood, clay, and stone and braced by vertical piling; small natural islands were expanded into crannógs by the same method. Often they were protected by a simple wooden palisade or a stone breakwater. Crannógs consisted mainly of wood (*crannóg* literally means "wooden frame" or "box"); later, they were part stone as well. The first such structures date from the early Neolithic period, but the Irish continued to build crannógs well into the Middle Ages. Some crannógs were still being used as dwellings in the seventeenth century. Most of them could be reached only by boat, but some could be approached by a causeway lying just below the surface of the water; its markers could be removed easily in case of a siege.

Northwestern Ireland, with its many lakes, was an ideal region for this type of fortification, and many well-preserved crannógs can be found there. But there are also such structures in Ballinderry (Antrim) and in Lough Gur.

La Tène Art

The Celtic art of the Continent is evident in its purest form in two ornamental stones of extraordinary beauty, the stones of Castlestrange and Turoe (illus. 10, page 37). Their asymmetrical fish-bladder and spiral ornaments date from the last five centuries B.C. and are proof of the influence of the Continental Celts on Irish art. La Tène culture also influenced goldsmithing, but this art drew so heavily on the stock of Irish forms that there are no "pure" La Tène pieces.

Metalwork and Enamel

Metalwork was important in both Britain and Ireland. It reached its zenith in the early Iron Age. In Britain, scabbards and clasps especially were decorated with curvilinear ornaments of all kinds (S-curves, snail shapes, palmettes, and hairspring spirals). The Irish rapidly adapted Continental and British influences. Although their own concepts are readily apparent, the relationship to the British style is recognizable in curvilinear border designs on gold necklaces and bronze trumpets.

The blending of native forms and the asymmetrical elements common to the Celtic regions of the Roman Empire lends a unique character to these objects, which appear to be full of restless motion. Irish metalworkers also exhibited their remark-

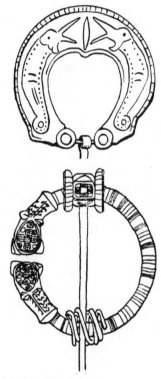

Fish-bladder and spiral ornament from the Turoe Stone, Galway.

TOP: *ring-shaped brooch;*
BOTTOM: *early spring brooch.*

Examples of early metalwork. CLOCKWISE, FROM TOP LEFT: *bronze cauldron; inlaid hook, perhaps used to suspend a sword; spearhead; gold* lunule *(necklace).*

Glass and porcelain ornaments.

Enameled bronze button and porcelain ornaments.

able skills in the production of light war chariots, whose use is attested to in tomb relics and in countless early sagas. This flowering of excellence was short-lived, however, as is revealed by several later armbands, which are quite crude and without ornamentation.

Another art form, enameling, persisted until well into the fourth century A.D. With the spread of La Tène culture, enameled objects, originally reserved for rulers' jewelry, became important all over Europe. Coral beads had been quite common in the third century. When they became scarce, glass buttons were substituted for them. These were replaced, in turn, by the first products of the enameling art. Even horse fittings came to be decorated with small spots of red enamel. Later artisans learned to use other colors as well, at first only in their purest form; for example, a number of Scottish armbands reveal a checkerboard pattern of yellow and red enamel. All these objects, like the ceramics of the period, were not produced in large, central workshops, but in self-sufficient farmsteads.

Ogham Script

The Ogham alphabet is known from roughly 300 inscriptions in Ireland (the majority in Cork and Kerry) and an additional 60 or so in Scotland and in Wales. It was used in writing the ancient Irish language; later, a number of the inscriptions were provided with Latin glosses. The script, similar to runes, was used between the fourth and seventh centuries A.D., well into the Christian period. Roman half-uncials replaced it. The symbols of the alphabet, which was named after Ogmios, the Celtic god of writing, were developed as follows. A series of short lines (one to five constitute a letter) was chiseled on either side or across the edge of a standing stone. Inscriptions (most of which consist of the names of a man and his father) begin at the bottom of the stone and read upward; they may run across to another edge and continue downward along it (illus. 18 and 19, page 40).

Vowels were represented by either horizontal cuts across or notches on the imaginary base line of the stone's edge. Consonants were chiseled as horizontal lines to the right, to the left, or diagonally across the base line.

Each letter of the Ogham alphabet derives from a Gaelic word for a tree or some other plant—for example, b = beith (birch), d = dair (oak), and f = fern (alder). The Picts of Scotland used it into the ninth century, as demonstrated by an inscribed stone

The twenty characters of the Ogham alphabet.

from Aberdeenshire. Selected symbols were still used in the Middle Ages. Under the influence of Christianity, many inscriptions from the Celtic period were either obliterated or "baptized" by the addition of a chiseled cross.

THE EARLY CHRISTIAN ERA

Ireland was one of the few parts of Western Europe to remain free of the domination of the Roman Empire, but it was fragmented by violent inner feuds. The south was ruled by the Eoghanacht dynasty, and Tara, in the north, was the seat of the O'Neills. Until Brian Ború seized power in 1002, these clans provided the country's high kings. Only scanty documents survive from the fifth century A.D., and these are too full of contradictions to be of great value to scholars. Still, it is clear that the island began to be converted to Christianity when St. Patrick arrived.

This great saint continues to be an enigma; perhaps this in itself is one of the reasons the Irish particularly revere St. Patrick, who, both a mystic and a practical man, so well understood their occult bent. In his last years, the saint wrote down the story of his life, and while his *Confessio* does provide historians with a number of details, it leaves far too much unexplained.

The first sure date in Irish history is the year 431. It was then that Pope Celestine I dispatched Bishop Palladius to Ireland to bring the sacraments to the faithful. What became of Palladius is not known. It is possible that he and St. Patrick are the same person, or perhaps his deeds have been ascribed to the more famous man. In any case, Palladius has been forgotten in Ireland, while St. Patrick has been venerated continuously since his own day. The annals give two dates for the death of St. Patrick, 461 and 493, and his arrival in Ireland is placed in roughly

432. Legend has it that the chief of the O'Neill clan frequently conducted raids that took him as far as Britain and Normandy and that he returned from one of these forays with a Christian, Latin-speaking youth named Patrick, whom he sold into slavery. Patrick thus exchanged his home in Roman Britain for the hills of Antrim, where he was set to

Map showing religious houses in Europe with which the Irish monasteries were closely connected.

watch over his master's herds. Eventually, following a divine inspiration, he escaped from servitude and secured passage on a merchant ship to Gaul, then full of unrest due to the fall of Rome and incursions by Germanic peoples. The young man rapidly made up for his lack of education and went to study in Lerins, where he became familiar with the rules of the Coptic monasteries. He then traveled through Italy and later returned to Britain.

After having been ordained a bishop, Patrick left Britain for Ireland, with a small party of followers, hoping to convert its heathen population to Christianity. In 433, Patrick is supposed to have lighted the Easter fire on the hill of Slane and immediately thereafter to have received permission from the high king to preach the gospel. The Irish willingly, even eagerly, took to the saint's teachings. As an old man, St. Patrick could report in his *Confessio* that the entire Irish population had been converted.

Thanks to St. Patrick's strong personality, the island had been converted with astonishing speed. Therefore, the Irish monks began to direct their proselytizing ambitions toward other shores. They were inspired by the example of ascetic desert saints and accepted the biblical injunction that staying too long in one spot can only cause the body and the mind to grow lax. Some monks therefore began to emigrate to the Continent in the sixth century. Generally setting out in groups of twelve, they made their way first to Rome and then to the deserts of Egypt. But even while still in Gaul, they urgently preached against the moral decline of the collapsing Roman Empire. These "pilgrims for Christ" came to be known by the Latin word for the Irish, "Scoti." They must have presented a miserable appearance when they arrived at the Frankish courts in ragged clothing after days of travel with virtually nothing to eat.

A number of parties also set out onto the uncertain vastness of the ocean, and Irish graves as far away as Greenland are not uncommon. In the *Peregrinatio Sancti Brandani*, a description of the adventures on one of St. Brendan's journeys, the most improbable assertions alternate with quite precise reporting, such as a detailed description of the life of the seal. Some of the monks sailed northward to the Shetland Islands and even to Iceland, while others set sail for Egypt. "Scottish" foundations—which were purely Irish establishments that added greatly to the strength and prestige of the Christian church—arose in many parts of Europe and as far east as Kiev.

St. Columba, also called Columcille ("dove of the church"), came from an ancient royal family. He was born in 521, the son of Felim and Ethne, from the royal houses of Aileach and Leinster, and is supposed to have been baptized in Temple Douglas (Donegal). The poetically gifted young nobleman founded his first monastery on the nearby Lough Gartan. Other foundations were to follow in Glencolumbkille (Donegal) and Kells (Meath), where a stone building still bears his name. While a guest at the monastery of St. Finian, on the island of Inishmurray, St. Columba secretly copied a manuscript that belonged to the head of that house. The high king commanded him to return the copy to St. Finian, but St. Columba refused, and a great battle ensued near Culdreime. St. Columba prevailed, but, grieving over the 3,000 deaths in this conflict, he took leave of his homeland and went to Scotland. There he founded the monastery at Hy, or Iona. Iona rapidly became a link to the culture of Europe, as is apparent from its manuscripts. The scriptorium of the monastery rose to particular prominence, and it is likely that the Book of Kells was created

Map showing the most important Irish monasteries.

there. When one of the Irish high kings threatened to limit the rights of poets and bards, St. Columba rushed home from Iona to champion them. Shortly afterward, in 597, the saint died at Iona.

St. Columban, or Columbanus, was a pupil of Comgal of Bangor. At the age of fifty, he determined to undertake a journey to visit the saints in the desert. In about 590, he and twelve companions arrived in the land of the Franks, at that time divided into three kingdoms and riven by bitter feuds. Queen Fredegunde reigned at Soissons, Queen Brunhild at Reims, and King Childebert at Autun. Childebert granted St. Columban permission to establish monasteries, and he promptly founded the communities of Annegray and Luxeuil. But Childebert's successor, Theodoric, drove St. Columban out of France. The saint followed the Rhine upstream, then crossed the Alps into northern Italy. There Agilulf, the king of the Lombards, presented him with a plot of land, near Pavia. On it, St. Columban founded his last monastery, Bobbio, where he died in

615. The oldest surviving Irish manuscript, the *Cathach*, or catechism, with quite simple initials and ornaments (illus. 25, page 42), was written by him.

Among those who set out with St. Columban from Bangor was a certain Gallus (St. Gall). He became ill along the way and stayed behind to build himself a small hermitage in the Alps. It was there that the powerful monastery of St. Gall was soon established. The first bishop of Salzburg, Virgilius (Latinized from Fergil), was an Irishman, and in a later wave of immigration, around 1150, the monk Marianus Scotus founded the "Scottish" monastery in Regensburg.

One of the great religious leaders who stayed in Ireland was St. Brigid. This highly venerated saint founded a double cloister for monks and nuns—separate, of course —near Kildare. Even here, the example of the hard life of desert fathers was followed, one full of renunciation and self-sacrifice. Monasteries of this period, such as the one at Clonfert, often counted as many as 3,000 monks and scholars. Their strength resulted from a broad program of instruction that included the study of Latin and Greek as well as of mathematics. Even the writings of Cicero and Horace were studied.

Several great schools of writing and sculpture attached to these monasteries gained an extraordinary reputation in Europe, and the preservation of Celtic culture is entirely due to the efforts of the Irish monks. Usually a new faith is loath to countenance even the smallest traces of earlier religious beliefs, but these monks showed themselves to be both worldly and generous. Still, they were firm in their faith; they accepted severe punishments for even the most trifling lapses, convinced that in doing so they were likely to come closer to God.

Only a few traces of this early monastic

life have been preserved, for the monks thought of themselves as wandering preachers and usually constructed their simple dwellings out of highly impermanent materials.

Irish monks stood out during the early Middle Ages because of the geographical extent of their missionary work—they ventured northward to Scotland and to the Faeroe Islands and southward to Italy and to the Egyptian desert—and the exemplary faith with which they determined to convert all of Europe. The Irish monks believed that knowledge of the arts and sciences —indeed, education in general—was desirable for its own sake and was pleasing to God. But they also disdained temporal power and earthly goods; they felt that these were likely to lessen one's compassion and subvert one's faith.

However, not all of the Irish monks ventured abroad. Many remained at home, whether in remote huts or in populous monasteries. The Irish people, who lived in loose tribes, soon settled in the vicinity of these monks, submitting to their teaching and relying on them for protection and security. In time, quite sizable communities grew up around the religious establishments, which came to constitute the intellectual and social centers of the country. The rigorous faith of the Irish has continued unbroken to the present day. For example, they still consider penitential pilgrimages numbering thousands of the faithful to be a matter of course.

Irish art and intellectual life became the chief civilizing factors of that era. They were extremely influential in shaping the art of Carolingian France and Germany. Like no other intellectual force, early Christian Ireland determined the course of a Europe taking shape amid the confusion of the Germanic migrations.

Architecture and Art of the Monastic Culture

The Vikings probably erected the first stone structures of any size in Ireland after their invasion in 795. On the east coast, they founded settlements and enlarged the towns they had conquered. Only after the Vikings had been thoroughly defeated in the battle of Clontarf in 1014 did the Irish actively build once more on their own. Although its wooden buildings were highly impermanent, stone remnants of the monastic culture have survived intact in numerous churches, round towers, and high crosses. And many examples of the art of monastic book illuminators also have been preserved.

Churches and Monasteries

The buildings from the early Christian period—both *clocháns*, dwellings built of

stones fitted together without mortar (illus. 15 and 16, page 39), and tiny churches that rarely exceeded 30 feet in length—give the appearance of beehives or overturned boats. Wooden churches preceded the stone ones,

A clochán.

Map showing Romanesque churches in Ireland.

vive the centuries. The Oratory of Gallarus (Dingle Peninsula, Kerry), modeled on a structure built of wattle, rises up in a simple curve from its foundations, resembling the graceful lines of a ship's hull (illus. 71, page 128). Carefully worked blocks of stone form a narrow gable, and joints between the stones are tilted to the outside so that water cannot seep into the interior.

Chapels constructed of wooden beams were also imitated in stone. In the seventh century, Cogitosus described a church that was divided into three sections and had many windows, and a tenth-century high cross that contained a depiction of a small chapel with a tile or shingle roof. This type of church is also represented in the Book of Kells and on various sarcophagi. One of the few such churches to have survived is on St. MacDara's Island, off the coast of Galway. Several buildings, such as St. Columba's House in Kells (illus. 69, page 128), contain a tiny upper story so low that one cannot stand up straight in it. Both types of churches described above had no ornamentation.

Early Irish monasteries were built within

and it would seem that two methods were used to build them. One was based largely on wattle; the other, on hewn beams. The first stone churches faithfully reproduced the designs of their forerunners, which is how scholars know anything at all about the wooden ones that have failed to sur-

Representation of the Temple of Solomon from the Book of Kells.

Early stone church near Illaun, on the island of St. MacDara, off the coast of Galway.

24

a circular enclosure and consisted of a number of beehive huts, which were the monks' cells, surrounding the church, the cemetery, and possibly a few workshops.

Round Towers

Some eighty round towers, either wholly or partially preserved, still indicate the locations of early monasteries.

Round towers, which began to be built in the ninth century, are the only purely Irish structures of this period. High crosses may also be found in Scotland, although there they are not so splendidly carved, and megalithic tombs are to be met with almost everywhere in Europe. But there are only a very few *cloigthithe* (singular *cloigtheach*, and Gaelic for "bell tower") outside Ireland, in Scotland and on the Isle of Man. In times of peace, the round towers were chiefly used to summon the monks by the ringing of hand bells. But the fact that the doors are placed from 10 to 15 feet above the ground suggests that they also served as places of refuge for monks and their treasures in times of distress; access was by means of wooden or rope ladders, which could be pulled up in the event of attack. Narrow and tapering toward the top, the round towers were divided into several stories, usually five, that were connected by ladders. The 65- to 110-foot towers were capped by conical roofs. The ratio of their base diameter to their height was generally 1:6. Narrow windows

ABOVE: *cross section of the round tower of Ardmore;* RIGHT: *round tower on Devenish Island.*

25

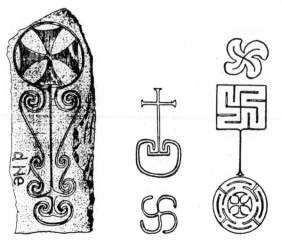

RIGHT: cross and spiral forms on the Reask Stone, Kerry; CENTER AND FAR RIGHT: examples of early Christian symbols on grave slabs, Cloon Lough, Kerry.

were placed so that one could survey a different segment of the landscape from each story. Firmly packed earth, often solidified with rocks, served as a foundation.

A clear stylistic development can be observed in the round towers. The roughly joined tower of Castledermot, from the tenth century, has no ornamentation, while later examples, such as those at Ardmore and Clonmacnoise, reveal notched joints, stone friezes, and doorways decorated in the Romanesque style.

In many of the cemeteries adjacent to the round towers, as at Clonmacnoise, there are quite unusual stones, early grave slabs, that constitute an artistic genre of their own. All varieties of forms of the cross can be found on them, from simple unornamented ones to the typically Irish shape with large, decorated ends. These stones date from the ninth to twelfth centuries and served a different function from that of the high crosses.

High Crosses

High crosses were not gravestones in the usual sense, although they are found mostly in the cemeteries of monasteries. Many of them bear an inscription that includes a request for a prayer.

Menhirs (illus. 9, page 37), which predate the coming of Christianity, and Ogham stones, to which crosses and Latin inscriptions were added during the early Christian period, were the forerunners of high crosses. In time, an entire stone block came to be carved in the shape of the cross and provided with ornamental borders. Beautiful examples of this early stage may be seen at Carndonagh (illus. 30, page 45) and Fahan (illus. 29, page 45), in Donegal.

From various reliefs, we know something of the use and form of wooden crosses that were used in processions. They were braced with quadrants and were ultimately translated into stone versions. Decorations from such wooden crosses, ornaments from metalwork, and illuminations from contemporary manuscripts served as patterns for the designs on ornamental crosses. This first form of true high crosses is represented by

26

the Slievenamon group, which is found only in southeastern Ireland and includes the Ahenny crosses (Tipperary) (illus. 34 and 35, page 47). Four quadrants of a circle connect the shaft with the arms and solidify the form. The material is soft sandstone, so easily worked that an uncommonly three-dimensional treatment of the ornamental fields on the shaft, arms, and ring was possible. Figures are represented only on the shaft in this early type of cross.

Bible crosses were designed to teach biblical stories and the meaning of the Christian doctrine to the largely illiterate populace. The cross ring, which doubtless also symbolized God's omnipotence, is smaller on these examples, which appear primarily on Ireland's central plain, than on the ornamental ones. Like the Slievenamon crosses, they are made of sandstone. Now, though, figures appear on all surfaces of the cross. The tall, narrow, rectangular shaft is divided into several compartments that display simple but quite affecting depictions of biblical scenes. Favorite and constantly recurring themes are Adam and Eve, Cain and Abel (illus. 44, page 116), the Miracle of the Loaves, and, as the embodiment of the monastic ideal, St. Anthony and St. Paul in the desert. Christ, either crucified or reigning in glory, often occupies the center spot (illus. 42, page 114). Neither the Annunciation nor the Nativity is ever depicted, however; but the Adoration of the Magi occurs a number of times.

In transitional forms leading from the ornamental cross to the Bible cross, such as the crosses at Kells (illus. 47, page 117) and Duleek, interwoven bands and animal motifs play an important role. Here, the shaft is not subdivided into compartments, although a number of scenes are shown, one above the other. The side panels of the shaft not only are covered with figures in

Map showing distribution of high crosses.

high relief but also boast vine and ribbon ornamentation.

In late Bible crosses, from the tenth and eleventh centuries, the shaft becomes more slender and graceful. These—the West Cross at Clonmacnoise (illus. 54, page 120) is an example—may stand as high as 20 feet. The ring is reduced in size, serving less as a brace than as an embellishment, and finally becomes only a faint recollection. The reliefs are strictly organized, and ornamentation has given way almost entirely to biblical scenes; a Romanesque sensibility is beginning to make itself felt. This style is represented by the crosses at Kells (illus. 47–49, pages 117 and 118), the West Cross at Clonmacnoise, and the Muiredach Cross at Monasterboice (illus. 41, 42, 44, 45, pages 113, 114, 116).

Along with the Bible crosses of the central plain of Ireland, there exists a related form with similar pictorial arrangements. The crosses at Moone (illus. 38–40, page 48), Kilcullen, and Castledermot (illus. 36 and 37, page 47) are carved from the local

Ruins at Clonmacnoise, Offaly, including a high cross.

The development of high crosses from the 7th to the 12th centuries.

Carndonagh, Donegal, 7th century.

Ahenny, Tipperary, 8th century.

Kells, Meath, 9th century.

hard granite of the Barrow Valley, in the southeast. The material itself necessitated a certain simplification and lower reliefs. The shaft is even longer than those of earlier crosses. Fabulous beasts, like those in the Slievenamon group, reappear, but these Barrow Valley crosses lack highly detailed ornamentation. Their loosely rolled spirals seem rather clumsy; the carvers may have begun their work without precise calculations or a spatial understanding of the whole because the last picture often has to make do with a smaller space and therefore looks cramped. The arrangement of many of the spirals intriguingly resembles designs that Mycenaean goldsmiths had done 2,000 years before. Figures are depicted in a highly styl-

ized and silhouetted form. The uniform, abstract representation of the twelve apostles (illus. 38, page 48) on the base of the Moone Cross is delightful in its disarming naïveté, as is the depiction of Daniel in the lion's den (illus. 40, page 48). The faces are absolutely rigid, suggesting astonishment or even fright.

Crosses from the eleventh century, like that at Drumcliff (illus. 55, page 120), no longer have any division into compartments. Ornamentation covers the greater part of the surface, and figures stand out from it in high relief. Finally, the late crosses, from the twelfth century, show a considerable change from traditional forms. The crosses at Kilfenora (illus. 58, page 121) and Dysert

Monasterboice, Louth,
10th century.

Drumcliff, Sligo,
11th century.

Dysert O'Dea, Clare,
12th century.

O'Dea (illus. 56 and 57, page 121) and several others on the Aran Islands, off the west coast, are hewn out of local limestone. Ornaments in the Ringerike style embellish these Aran Island crosses. Characteristic of this Scandinavian style from the early eleventh century is the representation of open, generally irregular leaves or vines with acanthus motifs. The latter design, a legacy from the late Roman Empire, consists of stemless leaves with notched or scalloped edges; it does not appear elsewhere in Ireland.

Near the cathedral at Kilfenora is a beautiful cross belonging to this late twelfth-century group, the Doorty Cross. It has a square base and only a single band of animal ornamentation below the Crucifixion; otherwise it is completely embellished with figures. The cross ring, although not pierced, has not yet been completely abandoned.

The cross at Dysert O'Dea is particularly striking for its sculptured figures of a crucified Savior staring straight ahead and of a bishop with mitre and staff in the Continental style. Intertwining serpents and other animals fill the base, and the ring has now completely disappeared. Crosses with Late Romanesque and Early Gothic characteristics may also be seen at Tuam, Cashel, and Glendalough.

The development of the high cross, with its birth, flowering, and decline, illustrates the typical course of an art form. A traditional object is suddenly given a new

—here Christian—stimulus, leading at first to quite simple forms of a new style. These become increasingly ornamented until they attain their most "baroque" culmination. Then, in time, they revert to the simpler, traditional forms from which they came.

Book Illumination

When the monks set out on their "pilgrimages for Christ" and began to preach the Christian gospel on the Continent, they often carried their most valuable possessions, their manuscripts, in caskets around their necks. Since no books from St. Patrick's time are preserved, it will never be possible to trace the development of this great bookmaking tradition completely. Art historians no longer view English and Irish book illumination as separate; they now know that the Irish Book of Kells and Book of Durrow were created during the same era as the English gospels of Echternach and Lindisfarne. St. Columba's monastery on the island of Iona, off the coast of Scotland, developed one of the foremost schools of book illumination, where Celtic and Germanic artistic currents converged and where Italian book illumination was known as well. But while the Italian school strongly affected the English tradition, it exerted only a slight influence on Irish artists. The magnificent forms of the Irish-Celtic style were fully developed in the earliest-known folios; later scribes working in the twelfth century were incapable of surpassing them. The coloring and ornamentation of the books of Durrow and Kells, from the seventh or eighth century, were never equaled.

The beauty of these gospels defies description. But some of the techniques by which they were produced are noteworthy. A minuscule script known as Insular half-uncial, derived from Latin script, was

Illuminated capital D in uncial form.

exquisitely penned on thick sheets of parchment in a very durable ink. Initials at the beginning of each of the gospels are made up of interlaced, highly ornamental designs that are at times bafflingly complex and that in some manuscripts, such as the Book of Kells, take up an entire page. The available surface is there given over entirely to decoration, with red lines bordering the separate bands of ornament. Many of the richer codices contain embellishments on pages without text and in the text itself.

The range of colors is limited to red, green, blue, and yellow; margins are whitened and backgrounds are shaded black. A consistent, uniform coloring is thereby achieved. The full, gleaming colors of the Book of Kells were often attained by painstaking application of successive layers of pigment. Ornamentation was generally restricted to depictions of the Evangelists, who are highly simplified, and their symbols. Faces and hands were left uncolored and unshaded. Gold and silver inks or colored parchments were not used.

In their illuminations, the Irish often used

32

1. Lough Nafooey at the foot of the Partry Mountains, near Leenaun, Galway.

2. Browne's Hill Dolmen, a cult burial site roughly 4,000 years old, Carlow.

3. Neolithic passage grave with main and side chambers, Loughcrew, Meath.

4. Squared stone passage to the burial chamber, Newgrange, Meath.

5. Burial chamber with sacrificial stone and spiral ornaments, Newgrange, Meath.

6. Spiral-ornamented capstone, Newgrange, Meath.

7. Poulnabrone Dolmen, Clare.

8. Bronze Age stone circle, Drombeg, Cork.

9. Early Christian stone near Reask, Kerry.

10. Turoe Stone near Bullaun, Galway, 3rd–2nd century B.C.

11. Boundary stone, Knowth, Meath.

12. Shaft of a high cross (10th century) and church ruins, Clonca, Donegal.

13. Single figure, White Island, Fermanagh (Northern Ireland).

14. Eight stone figures (c. 9th century) on White Island, Lough Erne, Fermanagh (Northern Ireland).

15. Skellig Michael, the rocky island off the coast of the Iveragh Peninsula, Kerry. In the distance, Little Skellig, the "bird island."

16. Group of beehive houses, Skellig Michael, Kerry.

17. Upper portion of the staircase (about 700 steps) on Skellig Michael, Kerry.

18. Stone with Ogham script, National Museum, Dublin.

19. Ogham stone, Kilmalkedar, Dingle Peninsula, Kerry.

20. Tara Brooch, c. 700 A.D. Diameter of the ring: 23 inches. National Museum, Dublin.

21. Tara Brooch (detail). Filigree tracery, spiral and animal ornamentation.

22. Ardagh Chalice, early 8th century. Height: 7 inches. National Museum, Dublin.

23. Ardagh Chalice (detail).

24. St. Patrick's Bell Casket, 11th century. National Museum, Dublin.

25. Cathach of St. Columba (detail), late 6th century. Library of the Royal Irish Academy.

26. Book of Kells, representation of Christ. Trinity College, Dublin.

27. Book of Kells, Virgin and Child. Trinity College, Dublin.

28. Early Celtic cult stone, 7th century, Boa Island, Lower Lough Erne, Fermanagh (Northern Island).

29. Ornamented standing stone with suggestion of cross arms, 7th century, Fahan, Donegal.

30. St. Patrick's Cross, the oldest high cross in Ireland, Carndonagh, Donegal.

31. Remains of a monastery complex, 6th century, Inishmurray, Sligo.

32. Small ornamented cross, Kilfenora, Clare.

33. North Cross, east face with ornamented fields, Ahenny, Tipperary.

34. Shaft of the North Cross, Ahenny, Tipperary.

35. South Cross, 8th century. Height: 10 feet, 9 inches. Ahenny, Tipperary.

36. South Cross, east face, 9th century, Castledermot, Kildare.

37. North Cross, west face, 11th century, Castledermot, Kildare.

38. Stylized depiction of the Twelve Apostles on the base of the Moone Cross, Kildare, 9th century.

39. Moone Cross, from the southeast.

40. Daniel in the lions' den, a frequent theme on the high crosses, depicted on the base of the Moone Cross.

Coptic, Syrian, and Armenian patterns and symbols, probably learned from Syrian merchants who brought fabrics, enamels, and ivory work to the island. Such "Eastern" motifs were so completely transformed and elaborated by Irish artists, however, that it would be inaccurate to speak of a direct importation of a style. Although many decorative motifs in Irish manuscripts are identical to those of other cultures, often much older ones—Mycenae, for example— it has so far been impossible to prove any ancient connection to Greece or to the Near East. Many ornaments, such as the sun circle, spiral, and double spiral, were native Irish forms. The trumpet pattern may have been modeled after the Roman palmette. This ornament, with its reminiscences of palm leaves and trumpet shapes, strongly emphasizes a central line, with a symmetrical arrangement of details on either side. But the dominant ornament in Irish illuminations is the interwoven band, which appears in all imaginable variations from circular forms to meandering strips. Representations of animals are often combined with such elements, producing a style that is typically Celtic-Irish. (Similar animal ornamentation occurs in eleventh-century Scandinavian art as part of the Urnes style.)

As a rule, the scribe and the illuminator were one and the same, and the names of a number of these artists have come down to us. The scribe who wrote the Book of Durrow closes his text with these words: "I pray to Your Majesty, Blessed Father Patrick, that whoever takes up this book might think of me, the scribe Columba, who wrote it out, with the grace of God, in a period of twelve days. Pray for me, my brother; the Lord be with you." Other known scribes were Ultan (died 655); Assicus, bishop of Elfin; and Dagaeus, abbot of Inniskeltra (died 587).

Examples of spiral and animal ornamentation from the Book of Durrow.

Human figures from the Book of Kells.

Animal ornamentation and depictions of animals from the Book of Kells.

The Great Books

The earliest extant Irish manuscript is the catechism, or *Cathach*, of St. Columba, from the late sixth century. Now displayed in the Royal Irish Academy in Dublin, the manuscript uses not only the script common to that period, a half-uncial with strongly accentuated rounding and horizontal serifs, but also the tentative beginnings of an original style of ornamentation (illus. 25, page 42). Red and brown inks were used for these designs—the same colors that form the text. Following each large initial, embellished with simple flourishes and snaillike forms, the letters become progressively smaller until the actual height of the text line is reached.

The Codex Ambrosianus D-23, created in Bobbio, already exhibits the prominent characteristic of Irish books—whole pages that are richly ornamented. Rosettes distributed among the interlacing are painted in red, dark green, blue, and yellow. Dotted outlines suggest the influence of the Coptic style. The artists of this book also adapted a number of motifs from contemporary metalwork.

According to its closing comment, quoted above, the Book of Durrow is a copy—certainly not the original—of a gospel written by St. Columba himself. In the seventh century, Durrow was more closely connected to Lindisfarne in England than to nearby Clonmacnoise. Thus the artist, doubtless an Irishman, was bound to be influenced by the English style of book illumination. At that time, a blending of the Old Latin versions of the gospels with that of the Vulgate—the revised translation of the Bible begun by St. Jerome in the fourth century—was in common use. Yellow, green, red, and a blackish brown dominate the ornamental pages that precede each of

Animal ornamentation from Irish gospels. 1–2. Book of Durrow; 3. Book of Kells; 4–5. Lindisfarne Gospels.

50

the gospels, which carry simplified symbols of the four Evangelists. Animal ornaments are found on many pages. Design motifs are borrowed in part from common objects. Hairspring spirals connected by trumpet shapes embellish one whole page. Multicolored patterns are made up of animal forms, plant motifs, and crosses, and the human figures are depicted in a naïve manner. Interlaced patterns are often outlined with double lines and are divided into smaller compartments. The Book of Durrow clearly exhibits the three elements that were characteristic of the Insular style of the seventh and eighth centuries: a Mediterranean-Coptic one, an Anglo-Saxon–Germanic one, and the Irish-Celtic one itself.

Aldred, a scribe of the tenth century, reports that Bishop Eadfrith of Lindisfarne (698–721) created the Lindisfarne Gospels, which are now in the British Museum in London. In about 640, King Oswald of Northumbria invited some monks from Iona, where he had been granted refuge for a time, to found a monastery on the east coast of his kingdom. St. Aidan accordingly set out with twelve brothers and founded Lindisfarne. The monastery soon became a center for the faith and a link between the cultures of Ireland and the Mediterranean, and it came under the sphere of influence of the Roman church, as represented by the archbishop of Canterbury. The Lindisfarne Gospels show obvious parallels to the Book of Durrow. Some of the decorations are more elaborate: in this English manuscript, the spirals, based on metalwork designs, are combined with the animal ornaments; the bands of interlacing are thinner than those of the books previously discussed; and the animals are not depicted in the same rough, Germanic style of drawing. The representations of the Evangelists are sculptural and highly detailed, even to the folds in the garments; in their posture, the Evangelists are somewhat reminiscent of figures in the Byzantine mosaics of the church of San Vitale in Ravenna. The scroll in St. John's hand foreshadows the Manesse Minnesang manuscript from the thirteenth century, and the slender, straight strokes of the initial pages point toward later Gothic scripts.

The Echternach Gospels are a product of the same school that created the Lindisfarne manuscript; its austere forms, however, are closer to those of the Book of Durrow. This manuscript once belonged to St. Willibrord, the abbot of the monastery at Echternach, in Luxembourg.

By far the most beautiful and important work of the Irish genius is the Book of Kells (illus. 26 and 27, pages 42 and 43), now in the Trinity College Library in Dublin, which was produced roughly a hundred years later than the two English manuscripts just described. According to the most recent scholarship, the Book of Kells may have been written in the Pictish region of Scotland and brought to Iona. Its style blends elements from a number of cultural traditions and is unique in the history of European book illumination. The embellishments are closely tied to the Irish tradition, although the text itself shows a similarity to writings of the Carolingian school, which would come into full flower at the court of Charlemagne. English influence, via the Lindisfarne Gospels, can also be recognized, as can the Mediterranean-Coptic origin of many of the ornaments. Out of these disparate elements, a completely independent entity was created, a magnificent manuscript rich with ornamental pages and skillfully executed even in its smallest details. On almost every page, next to the text block, there are small drawings of animals, people, or everyday scenes, often unrelated to the text. Preceding each gospel is an

ornamental page that incorporates a portrait of the Evangelist with his symbol. This is followed by an initial page that contains only a single letter. The Book of Kells also includes a series of pictures from the life of Christ, among them the Virgin and Child (illus. 27), the Temptation, and the Arrest. A final page is devoted to the four symbols of the Evangelists: enclosed in glorious bands of ornament are the transfigured man, or angel, of Matthew; the almost unrecognizable winged lion of Mark; the winged calf of Luke; and the eagle of John.

Human figures in the book appear somewhat awkward and naïve. They are treated not as portraits but as subordinate elements to the overall decorative scheme. However, the astonishing precision and diversity of the ornamentation are quite dizzying. The ornamental pages are as richly designed as a carpet, and individual details can scarcely be appreciated in such profusion. Spiral motifs, in which the primary colors are ennobled with purple, alternate with interlacing ornaments of incredible complexity.

The text is in an exquisitely beautiful half-uncial, often embellished with rows of dots, and is wonderfully suited to the design of the whole. The elegant letters stand close together, considerably more compressed than those of the Lindisfarne Gospels. The text alone could stand as one of the most beautiful surviving testaments to the culture of the early Middle Ages.

Beginning with the first forays of the Normans into Northumbria, more and more Irish fled back to their homeland, and thus the Book of Kells was removed from Iona to the monastery at Kells (Meath), where it was preserved until the secularization of that house.

Other Irish manuscripts can be found among the holdings of the great libraries of Europe. St. Gall's Stiftsbibliothek preserves several more elaborate examples from the Lindisfarne school. Until well into the eighth century, St. Gall manuscripts were marked with the Irish spirit and style. But then, under Othmar, a German, the rules of the Benedictine order were introduced into the monastery, and its old Celtic tradition gave way to more rigid organization. Most of the monks were native to the surrounding region and associated with another important Continental establishment, Reichenau, on an island in Lake Constance. In St. Gall MS 51 (c. 750–760) details and ornaments in the Mediterranean style are no longer so important. A calmer rhythm governs the framing bands of its pages, and the sculptural quality of the figures, which fill nearly the entire page, is less evident than in the Book of Kells, ushering in a new two-dimensional feeling.

Grimalt, the chaplain to Louis the German, was named abbot of St. Gall in about 840. He brought a number of Frankish-Carolingian influences to the monastery, and he championed the illumination of books. Codex 367 (c. 850) in the St. Gall Stiftsbibliothek clearly reveals the incorporation of Carolingian pictorial ideas. Animal forms are here worked into the forms of letters for the first time. Along with this book, a collection of gospel texts arranged to reflect the church year, a St. John Gospel (MS 60, Psalterium Aureum), the anthology MS 1395, and fragments of other gospels comprise the showpieces of the chapter library.

A gospel in the Hereford Cathedral library is closely related to these St. Gall manuscripts. In style it could be an earlier work by the master of St. Gall MS 51.

The National Library in Vienna houses the Cutbercht Gospel, which takes its name from its scribe's, of whom nothing further is known. It belongs to the southern English school and is executed in a delicate, expanded script that occupies only the right half of each page. The left-hand columns are embellished with initials, some of which are as much as 28 inches in height, comprised of ribbon ornaments and intertwining animals in geometrical arrangements. These decorations appear to be somewhat looser and less intricate than their Insular counterparts.

One of the chief works from St. Gall, the Folchard Psalter (Vienna) reveals a new type of more architectural letter that is provided with border ornaments of its own. This work introduces a new period and belongs to the Germanic style.

In addition to its more famous treasures, Trinity College Library owns a number of later codices, such as the Book of Mulling and the Book of Dimma. The Book of Mac-Regol, in the Bodleian Library at Oxford, is based on the ornamental tradition of the Book of Kells; it incorporates all of the latter's formal elements but fails to achieve a style of its own. A similar decline in style, this time as the result of adaptation to the Nordic tradition, is visible in MS B-II-30 of the cathedral library in Durham. The Royal Library in Stockholm preserves a Codex Aureus that, although strictly divorced from the Celtic element, is somewhat related to the tradition of Lindisfarne, and also shows parallels to both MS Barberini Lat. 570 in the Vatican Library and the Book of Cerne in the University Library at Cambridge. Additional Irish manuscripts can be seen in the Biblioteca Nazionale, Turin; the Bibliothèque Nationale, Paris; the Lambeth Palace Library and the British Museum, London; and the university libraries of Würzburg and Leyden.

THE MIDDLE AGES AND RENAISSANCE

Architecture of the Middle Ages and Renaissance

Churches

The Irish were finally able to quash the Vikings, who plundered St. Columba's monastery at Iona in 795 and began to settle in Ireland around 840, with the victory of the high king Brian Ború in the Battle of Clontarf in 1014. They thereby avoided becoming a Norse colony. The Vikings had plundered monasteries and ravaged the countryside; but they also established new settlements, and a number of huge structures survive as examples of their monumental architecture (illus. 78, page 181). During the ensuing period of peace, the Irish reconstructed.

But the twelfth century brought with it the most profound change for the island since the coming of Christianity: church reforms emanating from Rome led to the foundation and growth of a number of new monastic orders. Cistercians, Augustinians, Dominicans, and Franciscans would soon provide a new stability to people all over Europe. Rome's decrees effectively centralized the power of the church, putting an end to Ireland's independent monastic culture. Once the English had been con-verted, the archbishops of Canterbury began to take an active interest in the Irish church and claimed to have jurisdiction over it. In 1093, St. Anselm, then archbishop of Canterbury, wrote to the king of Munster, warning that abuses of dogma would have to cease, among them the practice of divorce. The high king Muiredach Ua Braian (Muircheatach O'Brien) was an active champion of church reform, and among the many donations he made to the church was his own royal seat of Cashel (Tipperary).

Early monastic building in Ireland had had no influence on the architecture of the Continent. On the contrary, it was only the Romanesque influence from the mainland that finally awakened an interest in architectural form among the Irish. Up to that time, as we have seen, the Irish monks had placed no importance on structural permanence. But when St. Benedict called for a *"stabilitas loci,"* a durable architecture rooted in its surroundings became acceptable to them. Irish architects and stone-carvers reveal themselves to have been open to the Romanesque style, combining it with their own imaginative forms and traditions. The portals and choir vaulting of their churches are decorated with splendid embellishments that resemble manuscript illuminations. Interwoven designs that incorporate stylized animals and ornaments were the favored decorative motifs. The first church in this style was Cormac's Chapel (at Cashel, Tipperary) (illus. 87, page 186), which was commissioned by Cormac MacCarthy, king of Desmond (present-day County Cork) and bishop of Cashel. Cormac summoned architects and stonecutters from all over Ireland as well as master masons from Germany and Britain who used the recently constructed cathedrals at Hereford and Canterbury as their models. Cormac's Chapel was dedicated in 1134, and other churches of the same type were soon built, especially in southern Ireland. Since the basic structural forms were often misunderstood or forgotten, stonecutters increasingly strayed from the Romanesque style of the Continent. They devoted their energies and fantasies to ornamentation instead, so that an Irish Romanesque arose. It is characterized by a simple rectangular ground plan, a steep stone roof, a choir arch, and beautifully ornamented arches over doors and windows. In the early thirteenth century, this maverick style became incorporated into the austere Early Gothic style of Cistercian architecture.

A synod held in Kells in 1152 gave the Irish church its first constitution. The country was divided into four archbishoprics and thirty-six dioceses. The archbishop of Armagh (Northern Ireland) became the primate of Ireland. But first it was necessary to break the hold of the island's traditionally separatist monasteries. On two trips to Rome, St. Malachy, the bishop of Armagh, met with Bernard of Clairvaux and urged him to send monks to settle in Ireland. Consequently, a handful of Cistercians arrived to build the first of that order's Irish monasteries at Mellifont (meaning "honey spring") on the banks of the Mattock (illus. 80 and 81, pages 181 and 182).

Countless kings and bishops attended the ceremonial dedication of this house in 1157. To the Irish, its architecture was bold and extraordinarily imposing. The church, some 200 feet long, was no longer merely surrounded by the separate huts of the brothers but rather incorporated into a large complex that included a refectory, a chapter house, cloisters, large dormitories, and kitchens. Other similar complexes were laid out even before Mellifont was completed, and by 1272, some thirty-eight had been built, among them Jerpoint, Holycross, Kilkenny, Boyle, and Kilcooly.

The Augustinians arrived near the close

Entrance to Cormac's Chapel, Cashel, Tipperary.

Interior of Cormac's Chapel, Cashel, Tipperary.

of the twelfth century and built their own foundations at Cong, Athassel, and Ballintober. Donal Mor O'Brian, the king of Thomond and an extraordinary patron of church building, made large donations to this order. Franciscans and Dominicans followed in the first half of the thirteenth century. In the fifteenth century, the Franciscans expanded countless monasteries and churches, such as Muckross, Ennis, Askeaton, and Rosserk, in the Irish Gothic style and founded new abbeys. Battlements on top of slender towers are typical features of this style. Among the most important examples of Gothic architecture are Christ Church Cathedral and St. Patrick's Cathedral, both in Dublin. Each has served as Ireland's chief cathedral at various times.

Sculptured tombs and baptismal fonts also reveal the decisive influence of English art and architecture.

Styles changed in the course of time and became so dependent on English examples that no uniquely Irish art survived. Ireland's medieval tombs, however, compare quite favorably with those of England and the Continent. Generally built into the side wall of a church nave, such tombs consist primarily of a stone sarcophagus whose sides are ornamented with sculptures of the apostles or scenes from the lives of the saints. Graves in the walls themselves or in the floor are covered by large stone slabs, usually bearing Gothic inscriptions in Latin. Tombs from the thirteenth and fourteenth centuries commonly incorporate likenesses of bishops or knights; on the sarcophagi of the fifteenth through seventeenth centuries, wives are often depicted lying beside their husbands. Especially beautiful tombs were created by one distinguished family of stonecutters, the O'Tunneys. The most gifted of them was Rory O'Tunney, who is responsible for the cloisters at Jerpoint Abbey and the tomb of Piers Oge Butler in Kilcooly Abbey.

Baptismal fonts also constitute some of the country's sculptural masterpieces. Those in Meath and Westmeath are particularly noteworthy. Also significant is a new type of stone cross that is found along roadsides to commemorate a notable person or event.

Castles

Along with the churches of the various monastic orders, Ireland's castles, built mostly by the English, survive as the country's most imposing architectural monuments.

The first castles in Ireland were built at the time of the first attacks by the Anglo-Normans, who rapidly erected fortifications with which to secure their conquests. A wall of earth flattened at the top and often surrounded by a moat protected their huts and houses. High wooden towers standing within a curve of the wall crowned these fortresses. None of these have survived, but one can still explore the grass-covered walls at Ardscull, Callan, and Granard.

Much later, in about 1200, when half of Ireland was in Anglo-Norman hands, the conquerors recognized that the existing fortifications were inadequate to control their holdings. Therefore they set about building castles in their native style. These square fortresses, strengthened by towers at their corners and roofed with shingles, must have made a great impression on the Irish. Surrounded by tall, crenelated walls that incorporated several round towers, the Norman castles provided maximum protection for their inhabitants. From a description of Swords Castle in 1326, one can see how similar it was to Continental fortresses. The castle had a large main hall with a fireplace in the center, kitchens and pantries, rooms for servants and guards, stalls, and a bakery. The best-preserved fortresses from this period are those in Trim (illus. 73, page 178), Adare, and Athenry. The English continued to construct these castles until well into the fifteenth century, yet Irish builders rarely imitated them. The O'Connors of Connaught were among the few who perceived the military advantages of such a layout; in about 1300, they became the first Irish family to build a Norman-style fortress from which to carry on the struggle against the English.

Carrickfergus Castle, Antrim.

During the fourteenth century, there were a number of skirmishes between the Irish and the English, but since the rebels were not united among themselves they could not prevail. Almost no new fortresses were constructed during this period, though several were improved and expanded. Then in the fifteenth century, there was a surge of building of new castles and churches. Whole towns, such as Clonmines (Wexford), were surrounded by walls, and the building of new fortresses was officially encouraged. In 1429, Henry VI proclaimed that he would contribute £10 to anyone building a castle; at that time, this was a considerable sum —one that could buy a sizable estate. The dwellings of the Irish in this period were smaller than those built a century earlier. They had arched roofs and living quarters that were anything but commodious. Various travel descriptions, such as that of the Frenchman Boullaye de Gouz, provide quite accurate information about them. Their walls were pierced by only small windows, narrow slits that admitted very little light into the gloom. Beds were cots that tended to be covered with rushes, or with straw in winter. Rushes were also strewn ankle deep on the floor; sanitation was obviously not superior. Furnishings may have been primitive, but pantries and cellars were generally well filled, and Irish hospitality was just as exceptional then as it is now.

Between 1450 and 1650, simple multi-storied towers were built in a number of parts of Ireland as fortified dwellings. Projecting smaller towers at their corners served as stairwells. The smooth walls of these massive square towers provided such excellent protection that outer walls like those at Trim Castle could be dispensed with. Late castles of this type have survived at Bunratty and Blarney. Soon they gave way to the English Tudor style.

As defense became less essential, the Irish began to build themselves spacious, imposing country houses and palaces like Ormond Castle in Carrick-on-Suir. Interiors with plaster decorations and oversized windows gave these two- and three-story houses a light and inviting air. The Irish, bound as they were to tradition, continued to build their tower fortresses.

THE STRUGGLE FOR INDEPENDENCE

In 1166, Dermot MacMurrough, king of Leinster, was overthrown for stealing another prince's wife, Devorguilla, and banished to England. Henry II supported his plan to reconquer his kingdom, but in return for the assistance of Anglo-Norman knights MacMurrough had to promise them grants of Irish land. Thus began the Anglo-Irish conflict that persists to this day. A vanguard landed in the shallow Bannow Bay, conquered Wexford from the land side, and there joined the main force of the Norman army in 1169. The commander of this force was Richard Fitzgilbert de Clare, earl of Pembroke, whom the Irish called Strongbow. In a short time, central Ireland as far north as Dublin had been overrun.

Many of the English knights who had been given tracts of land easily adapted themselves to the Irish way of life. Surrounding

Dublin, the district known as the Pale had been established. This area acquired a purely English culture and was a point of departure for later English attempts at conquest. Three-quarters of Ireland was now occupied, castles were constructed, and a central government was set up. Because the English barons waged wars against one another, the Irish managed to gain strength in a number of areas—the beginning of their long struggle for liberation.

In 1535, Henry VIII dissolved most religious establishments and claimed their properties for himself, so he could settle them on deserving members of the English nobility. A few monasteries escaped this fate, and some continued to exist in secret—but not for long.

Three major uprisings supported by the pope and by Philip II of Spain (1569–1573, 1579–1593, and 1594–1603) came to nought. A peace treaty was signed in 1604. The English Civil War split Ireland into several parties. The rule of Oliver Cromwell (1649–1660), who landed in Ireland with an army in 1649, was marked by plundering and destruction. The entire country was subjected to even stronger English control, which inspired in its people a profound hatred for the English.

In the eighteenth century, a Protestant minority was ruling over the Catholic majority. But in spite of restrictive clauses passed by Parliament in London, a certain degree of prosperity existed in the Anglo-Irish cities. London proclaimed the Union of England and Ireland. The Georgian style came to stamp the image of Ireland's cities and palaces. With the lifting of the Penal Laws in 1829, the Irish were given new hope for equality, but rapid population growth and the potato blight led to the catastrophic famine of 1845 to 1851, which claimed more than 1.5 million victims. A mass exodus began as thousands crowded onto ships sailing for the land of promise, the United States. In Ireland, militant units were formed to propagandize for the struggle for independence. In 1848 came the uprising known as Young Ireland. Land reforms in 1881 once more gave the Irish grounds for

Tombs, allegedly of Strongbow and his son, in Christ Church Cathedral.

A riot in a potato store during the great famine.

hope. The Gaelic League, a patriotic organization founded in 1893, attempted to preserve and revive Celtic traditions and, above all, the Irish language. Similar goals were espoused by the Sinn Féin movement begun in 1899.

The first labor unions were founded in the first decade of the twentieth century. A bill calling for Home Rule passed by the Irish Parliament in 1914 was in fact signed by George V, but was never enforced. A battle raged between the Irish Volunteers (republicans, nationalists) and the Ulster Volunteers (Protestants, labor unionists).

Events of World War I did little to interrupt these hostilities.

In 1916, the Easter Rebellion broke out; it was beaten down after days of bloody unrest and ended with the execution of its leaders and the deportation of the rebels. Because of these gruesome battles, the population began to think somewhat differently, and in the elections of 1918, Sinn Féin was given a rousing victory. A separate National Assembly was founded, and Éamon de Valéra was elected president. England declared martial law, and the Anglo-Irish War lasted from 1919 to 1921. After a truce was called

Starving peasants besiege a workhouse during the great famine.

on December 13, 1920, the Anglo-Irish Treaty was signed, creating the Irish Free State, a kind of dominion that did not include the six northern counties. During negotiations with the English over the treaty, the provisional Irish government split into two camps, the Republicans under de Valéra and the Free Staters under Michael Collins. The latter supported the division treaty with the English; the former strictly opposed it. A bitter civil war began. Michael Collins was assassinated, de Valéra had to go underground, and one Republican position after another was lost. Executions of the "Irregulars" (opponents of Home Rule) began. In April 1923, de Valéra finally regained control. Frank Aiken, the moderate new leader of the Irish Republican Army, ordered a truce on April 30, 1923. De Valéra was able to expand Ireland's independence. During World War II, Ireland maintained a policy of neutrality under its president, Douglas Hyde. The Republic of Ireland was proclaimed in 1949.

The beginnings of general prosperity, a gradual development of industry, and membership in the United Nations have given Ireland a new self-confidence. President John F. Kennedy's state visit was seen as a confirmation of the nation's independence. Yet events of recent years have left little hope for peace on the island until the struggle for the six counties still under British control can be laid to rest. Bitter guerrilla action erupts exclusively in Northern Ireland, and there primarily in the cities of Belfast, Londonderry, and Newry. Travel in the Republic of Ireland is quite safe.

IRELAND'S SAGAS AND POETS

To understand the history of Ireland and its present-day troubles, one must reach far back to the time when bards sang of the power and bravery of their kings and princes in poems that related stirring fates and momentous events. The virtues and ideals extolled in these songs and even the forms of the songs themselves already anticipate the later troubadours.

Only since the nineteenth century has scholarship begun to deal in earnest with early Celtic-Irish culture. Since no written documents survive in Ireland or in other Celtic countries, the sagas handed down unchanged for centuries by the *shanachies*, or storytellers, comprise our most important sources. Many of the *shanachies* could recite verbatim stories they had heard but once, decades before. Their sagas, which were first written down in the early Chris-

Becuma of the White Skin, who was banished from the Many-Coloured Land. (Arthur Rackham)

tian period, contain the most fantastic and improbable claims alongside detailed information about invasions, battles, and the origins of foreign peoples, whose wanderings are recounted minutely in many a chronicle. Thus scholars are able to make useful assumptions about the peoples mentioned in the sagas. Through the centuries, groups of people from western France and even from Greece had settled on the island. Comparison of burial sites also permits archeologists and historians to trace a connection to the Iberian Peninsula. The last immigrants, who arrived in roughly the fifth century B.C., were Goidels (Gaels), remains of whose settlements have been uncovered by archeologists.

Stories from this period speak of Milesians, Firbolgs, Picts, and various other peoples whose precise origins are unknown. One powerful race was the Tuatha dé Danaan, or people of the goddess Dana, who are described as having been godlike and versed in magic. But in spite of their superiority, they gave way to the Milesians, the next wave of immigrants, and ever since, legend

has it, they have lived as exiles in the remoteness of the mountains. Even today these spirits are said to abduct an occasional maiden and take her back with them to their own realm.

Belief in spirits is still quite strongly rooted in the Irish, especially among the country people. Heroes, gods, and spirits have always constituted the core of Irish saga, and elves particularly sparked poetic fancies until well into the nineteenth century. In 1825, the first volume of a book by T. C. Croker, *Fairy Legends of the South of Ireland*, appeared in London. Croker's knowledge of the land and its history was profound, and in the following year, his book was published in Germany, translated by the brothers Grimm. Their introduction to it includes a catalogue of the recurrent figures in the stories and their particular characteristics. The *shefro*, a cheerful sort, loves games, music, flowers, and the joys of life. The *leprechaun*, who is forever guarding buried treasure, is often shrewd and mischievous; he smites his enemies with stunning, even deadly, blows from his invisible

hand. The *cluricaun* is a clumsy lone wolf who plays dirty tricks on people, and he was among the first to know of the pleasures of tobacco and of the secret—supposedly brought to Ireland by the Danes—of brewing beer from grains. The *banshee*, a female spirit of distinguished lineage, only appears for the purpose of warning a family of the approaching death of one of its members. The *phuka* is the spirit of dreams; the person who touches him in one of his animal forms is suddenly spirited away on flights above the valleys, to the moon, or even under water—to Tir na n-Og, the delightful land of youth where time has no sway.

All of Ireland's sagas have been divided into a number of cycles and have been precisely categorized. The first, or mythological cycle, is rooted in the pre-Celtic tradition, and gods, heroes, and the land of youth—the hereafter—play important roles in it. The next, the Red Branch cycle, relates the deeds of the hero of the Ulanids, Cúchulainn. During this period, the political and cultural center of the country was Eamhain Macha, which today is a grass-covered fortification in Armagh (Northern Ireland). The hero's real name was Setanta, and the story of how he came to be called Cúchulainn is a favorite: Setanta's uncle, the king of Armagh, once invited the youth to a banquet as a reward for his skill at hurling, a ball game still much enjoyed by the Irish. The blacksmith was ordered to get everything ready for the feast but was not told of the additional guest. He therefore closed the heavy gates and unleashed his fierce dogs outside to protect the king. When Setanta arrived at the smithy, one of the dogs attacked him, and seeing no help forthcoming from the house, he took hold of the animal and killed it with his bare hands. Setanta was highly praised for his feat, but nevertheless the blacksmith complained about

the loss of his best dog. At that, the young hero vowed to serve as the blacksmith's dog until a new one could be found. And that is how Cúchulainn—the dog of Cullan—got his name.

The heroes of the third saga cycle were the Fenians and their leader, Finn MacCool. The Fenians were the soldiers of the high king in roughly the third century A.D. Each of them could give battle to nine enemy soldiers at a time, but they were also philosophers, poets, and solvers of riddles. Their strict code of ethics suggests a high level of culture and resembles the medieval courtly ideal: one was to treat women, children, scholars, and poets with honor and respect; toward the common people, one was supposed to be just and generous. The religious beliefs of this period acknowledged a direct connection to supernatural and subterranean worlds. Almost every Fenian had a mother, nurse, or sweetheart who had been spirited away by the Tuatha dé Danaan, the ancient people long since fled into the hills.

The bards wrote to celebrate occasions rather than to express sentiments. Their verses served to transmit information and to glorify the deeds of military heroes and kings. The poets fell into a number of ranks and enjoyed appropriate social standing. It was a very high honor, and one most difficult to attain, to be a poet of the first rank.

The monks began quite early to collect and write down such old Irish stories and to add new elements—mostly travel experiences—to them. One such collection is the *Imramha* (*Journeys*), which in part depicts actual historical events. Another is the *Imram Brain* (*Travels of Bran*), which served as the model for the famous *Navigatio Sancti Brandani*, or *Journey of St. Brendan*.

The Irish language continued to live on in literature even under English rule. Many poets, such as Owen Roe O'Sullivan in the

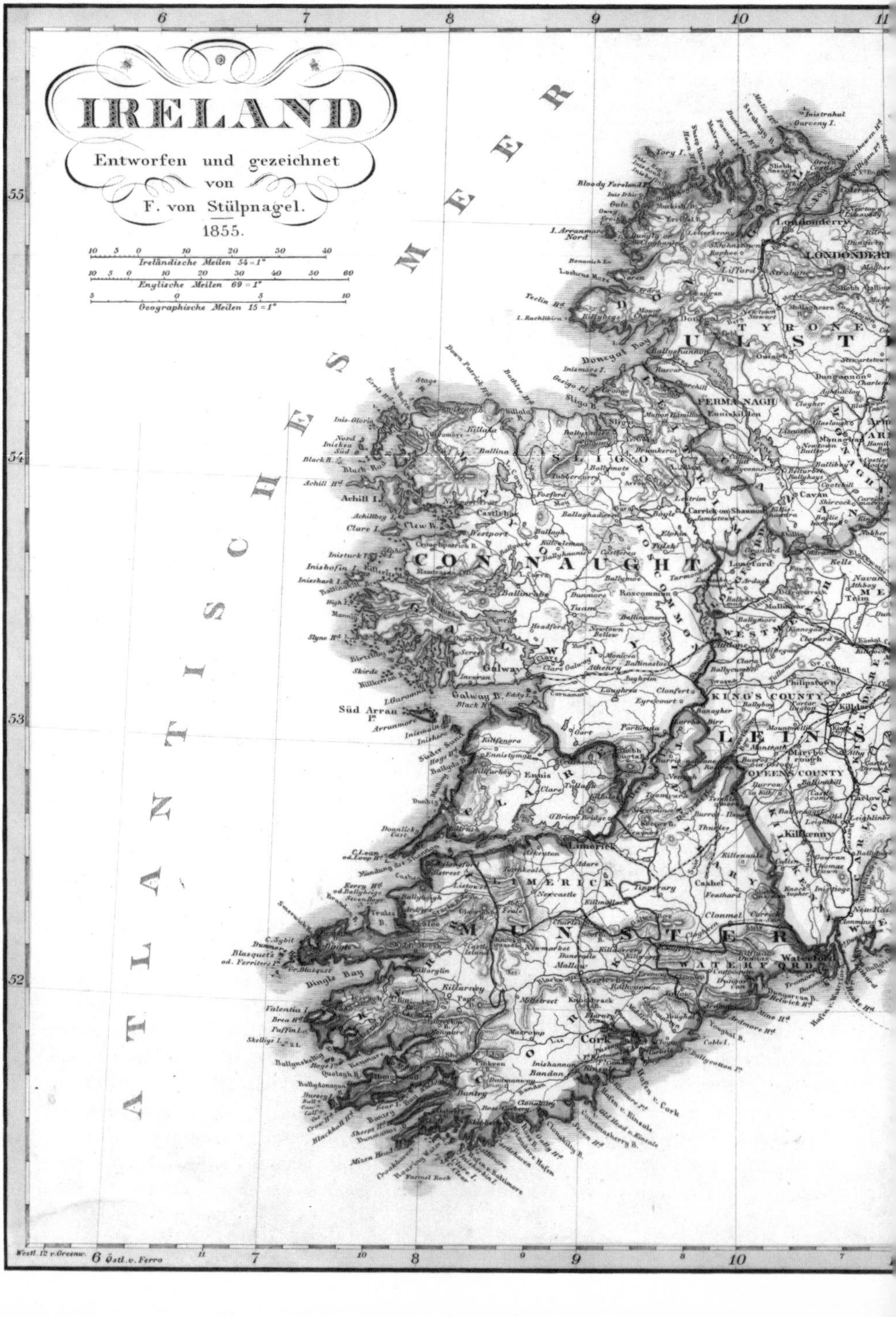

IRELAND
Entworfen und gezeichnet
von
F. von Stülpnagel.
1855.
Irländische Meilen 54 = 1°
Englische Meilen 69 = 1°
Geographische Meilen 15 = 1°
ATLANTISCHES MEER
CONNAUGHT
ULSTER
LEINSTER
MUNSTER
TYRONE
FERMANAGH
SLIGO
GALWAY
CLARE
LIMERICK
KING'S COUNTY
QUEEN'S COUNTY
WATERFORD
Londonderry
Donegal Bay
Galway
Galway B.
Süd Arran
Limerick
Tipperary
Cork
Waterford
Kilkenny
Bantry
Dingle Bay
Killarney
Ennis
Tuam
Roscommon
Westport
Castlebar
Ballina
Sligo
Achill I.
Clare I.
Valentia I.
Clonmel
Cashel
Mallow
Bandon
Youghal
Longford
Athlone
Philipstown
Westl. 12 v. Greenw.
Östl. v. Ferro

Map of Ireland from the
Stieler Hand'atlas, *1855.*

The abbot, who collected tales, from Mongan's Frenzy. *(Arthur Rackham)*

post-Cromwell period, earned their living as illegal, itinerant teachers of the language. Like the women who specialized in lamenting for the dead, they spoke mainly in verse. Indeed, the Irish generally combine words most artistically and effectively.

In the realms of music and painting, the Irish have never developed anything uniquely their own. But a distinctly quick wit and eloquence have continued to characterize the people up to the present, even though they have been using the English language since the eighteenth century. The last bard, Carolan O'Turlough, died in 1738 and left behind more than 200 Irish songs that number among the best of the genre. Yet the Irish have been able to handle English perhaps even more elegantly than Irish. Their fiction, verse, and drama have found a secure niche in world literature. Oliver Goldsmith, the master of Irish gallows humor, is deserving of mention, as are Oscar Wilde, George Bernard Shaw, Laurence Sterne, and, from this century, James Joyce,

Samuel Beckett, and Sean O'Casey. But probably no Irishman contributed so richly to the English language as did William Butler Yeats. His works are written in a realistic, vigorous style, and, like all Irish poets, he fills them with subtle wit and often highly pointed scorn. Yeats wrote his epitaph himself—he was buried in Drumcliff—and it serves as a splendid example of his style:

Cast a cold eye
On life, on death.
Horseman, pass by!

Ireland's eventful history and its struggle for freedom have been the subjects of countless poems like the following one by Patrick Pearse:

Christmas 1915

O King that was born
To set bondsmen free,
In the coming battle
Help the Gael!

A

JOURNEY
THROUGH
IRELAND

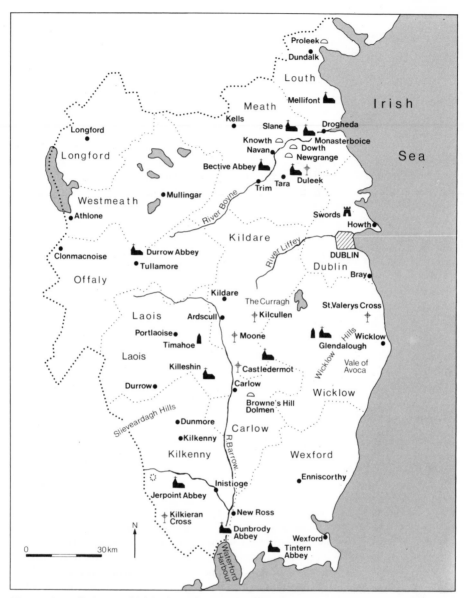

The province of Leinster, which includes the counties of Wexford, Carlow, Kilkenny, Laois, Kildare, Wicklow, Dublin, Offaly, Westmeath, Meath, Longford, and Louth.

LEINSTER

Even in early historical times, the southeast of Ireland served as the link between the island and Britain and the Continent. One of the most popular ferries sails from Fishguard, Wales, to Ireland's Rosslare Harbor. If one first sets foot on Irish soil here, one will easily see why the Irish call their homeland the "Emerald Isle." Beyond this gentle coastline are remarkable green pastures dotted with gorse bushes and flocks of sheep. Thanks to the hedgerows that border the lanes and crisscross the landscape, even the lack of trees does not immediately strike one. In "garden Ireland," there are scarcely any uncultivated spots, and the relatively high number of sunny days a year permits optimal use of the soil. The landscape here, as all over the island, gives an impression of cleanliness. The absence of refuse, heavy traffic, and billboards puts one in a holiday mood from the start. The towns are full of history; in fact, the smaller the town, the more tangible is the past.

Wexford

Wexford—Ferns—Enniscorthy —Clonmines—Tintern Abbey— Dunbrody Abbey—New Ross

Set on the funnel-shaped estuary of the Slaney, *Wexford* commanded a position that was virtually impervious to attack by sea. Therefore, the Anglo-Norman vanguard in 1169 landed in Bannow Bay, somewhat farther west, capturing the town, which had been fortified by the Vikings between the eighth and tenth centuries, from the land side. They thus smoothed the way for the main force, which was following in its ships. Although only fragmentary remains recall Wexford's history, the narrow, crooked streets still present a vivid picture of medieval life in the town. The massive Westgate Tower and the Bull Ring are evidence of the Norse monumental architecture and coarse amusements. Not far from this scene of noisy pleasures rise the ruins of Selskar Abbey, a foundation from the thirteenth century. Here, Henry II of England carried out his penitential fasts after the murder of Thomas à Becket in Canterbury Cathedral. A few centuries after the Normans, Cromwell massacred the town's defenders in Wexford.

Traveling northward one comes to *Ferns*, the former seat of the kings of Leinster. Here one finds impressive thirteenth-century fortifications, as well as the remains of an abbey founded in the sixth century for St. Maedhog. The cloister, with its chapel built in the style of Cormac's Chapel (Cashel), was given to the Augustinians in the twelfth century. The shaft of a cross supposedly indicates the grave of Dermot MacMurrough, who, when deposed as king of Leinster, first summoned the Anglo-Normans into Ireland. The Book of Leinster, one of the most important sources for early Irish history, was written in Ferns.

The powerful castle of *Enniscorthy*, with its four thirteenth-century towers, now houses a museum with artifacts from the Stone Age up to the present. Returning to the south coast, one comes upon the level beach of Bannow, which practically appears to invite invasion. Here, there are still remains of one of the first motte and bailey forts—trenches and walls that testify to the determination not to surrender the country.

Via *Clonmines* one comes to *Tintern Ab-bey*. The church is difficult to find; next to a farmhouse, a path closed by a gate leads from the road and across the fields. William le Mareschal, first earl of Pembroke, built this church in the twelfth century, in gratitude for a safe journey across from England. Its scenic surroundings may strike the visitor as being quintessentially Irish. A small stream winds between leafy banks shaded by willows, and horses graze next to the stump of an ancient round tower (illus. 91, page 189).

On the way to New Ross one passes *Dunbrody Abbey*, which was founded by Hervé de Montmorency, one of Henry II's marshals. He made himself abbot of this new cloister, a simple enough matter for an uncle of

Enniscorthy.

88

Dunbrody Abbey.

Strongbow, the English commander. In the fourteenth century, the monastery belonged to various owners until it was taken over by Cistercian monks. In 1537, it came into the possession of Henry VIII, who gave it to the first Irish bishop of the Reformation, Alexander Devereux. The cruciform church, one of the largest Cistercian buildings in Ireland, comprises a nave, choir, and transept. In the sixteenth century, a large central tower and a number of adjacent buildings were added, including a chapter house, housekeeping rooms, and a library.

New Ross, farther to the north, has a certain typical Irishness about it, and thousands of Americans a year make a pilgrimage here. New Ross is the ancestral home of the late John F. Kennedy, and at least since Kennedy gave his memorable speech before the Dail (the lower house) and the Senate he has been much admired in Ireland.

Kilkenny

Inistioge—Jerpoint Abbey—Kilkenny—Killeshin

Going northward from New Ross, one comes to *Inistioge*, whose church consists of only the choir and the central tower of the former Augustinian priory (illus. 90, page 189). The crenellated pediment of the west tower is typical of the fifteenth century.

Just west of Thomastown lies the Cistercian cloister *Jerpoint Abbey* (illus. 76 and 77, page 180). The setting for one of Shakespeare's comedies ought to look just like this. *Measure for Measure* or *Twelfth Night* could be staged here superbly. The figures on the Romanesque columns imply that sinning is only human, while those on the tombs look like the guests at a traditional

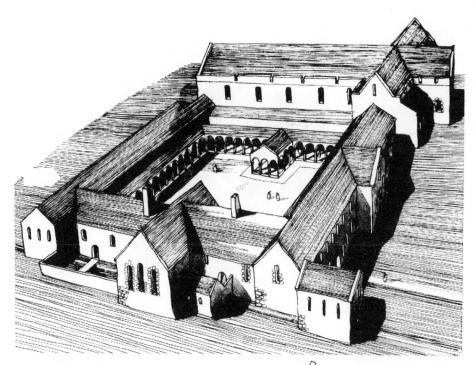

Reconstruction and ground plan of Jerpoint Abbey, Kilkenny.

1. *Entrance*
2. *Dormitory*
3. *Kitchen*
4. *Refectory*
5. *Common room*
6. *Cloister garden*
7. *Chapter house*
8. *Sacristy*
9. *Tower*
10. *Monks' choir*
11. *Lay brothers' choir*

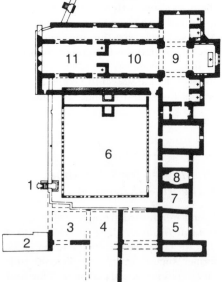

wake—after the mourning is over; now carousing, gluttony, boasting, and sloth are given full rein. Cheerful portraits of animals stand between men in religious garments. All of this work was created by the master sculptor, Rory O'Tunney. He also created the tomb of James Shortal in St. Canice's Cathedral in Kilkenny, but little else is known about him.

The generous, square layout of Jerpoint

Abbey is typical of Cistercian Gothic architecture. The church, with its aisled nave, occupies the north side, leaving the other three to housekeeping buildings, dormitories, and the chapter house. The eastern portion was constructed in 1160; the Gothic window is from the fourteenth century. All the rest dates from roughly 1180. The aisles of the church have a Gothic character, yet the structure as a whole is definitely Romanesque—note, for example, the round-arch windows along the west wall. In the center of the nave a screen separated the monks from the lay brothers. The tomb of Felix O'Dulany, bishop of Ossory (died 1202), and the sarcophagi of two knights lie close to the altar.

If one wishes to make the small side trip from Thomastown to *Callan*, one can discover a worthwhile Augustinian abbey and a motte (steep, flat-topped mound, once fortified and surrounded by a ditch). In the church of St. Mary, from the thirteenth century, there is still another work of O'Tunney's to admire, the tomb of John Tobyn.

One then approaches the pearl of southern Irish towns, *Kilkenny*. Hardly any other spot in Ireland is so impressive—not because of any specific works of art here, but because it is an inviting area, at the base of the Slieveardagh Hills and on the banks of the River Nore, that gives the visitor a special sense of the country and its tranquil way of life. Kilkenny Castle, the former seat of the Butlers of Ormonde, built by William le Mareschal, Strongbow's son-in-law in 1192, is reflected in the river. Its first layout was square, with round towers at the corners. Later additions, however, soften the fortresslike effect of this Romanesque establishment that replaced the ancient royal seat of Ossory. The Butlers of Ormonde were one of the clans most loyal to the Stuarts in the seventeenth century. They supported Charles I and brought an end to Cromwell's rule.

Kyteler's Inn, the oldest building in Kilkenny (fourteenth century), houses a historic tavern with interiors from the seventeenth century. They still tell here of a hostess from centuries ago who supposedly murdered four successive husbands, was then accused of witchcraft, and fled to the Continent.

St. Canice's Cathedral, the second largest church on the island, was originally part of a Romanesque abbey (illus. 83 and 84, page 183). Founded in 1251 by Bishop Hugh de Mapilton as a fortress church, it is a superb example of the early English style. The glass windows of the choir were famous far and wide, but they were smashed in by Cromwell's soldiers. Today, a number of lancet windows and many gravestones by Rory O'Tunney still testify to the extreme skill of its architects and stonecutters. There are artistically carved tombstones not only of members of the Ormonde family, but also of master craftsmen. One of the stones is inscribed in Norman French. It is possible to climb the old round tower next to the church on payment of a small entrance fee.

St. Canice's Cathedral.

Doorway of the church of Killeshin.

The next important stop is the church of *Killeshin* in County Laois. St. Comghan founded a monastery here—a spot with a panoramic view over the Barrow Valley and the Wicklow Mountains beyond it—near the close of the fifth century. The settlement was repeatedly attacked; the chapel was destroyed in 1041, and a fire leveled the entire monastery in 1077. The present church, founded in 1160 by Dermot MacMurrough, boasts a well-preserved Romanesque doorway made of light and dark sandstone blocks (illus. 96, page 192). Like all true Irish doorways, it is constructed of wedge-shaped stones fitted together, rather than square stones with wedge-shaped joints. The inscription on the doorway, "A prayer for Diarmait, King of Leinster," permits it to be dated with some accuracy, for Diarmait (Dermot) died in 1117. The doorway is composed of four pairs of columns, each set slightly behind the other, whose shafts and capitals are embellished with ornaments and stone heads. Each pair supports a round arch, and the arches become progressively smaller toward the door itself. The keystone of the outermost and largest arch carries a stone face whose stylization shows a definite Celtic influence. The unornamented, pointed gable also rests on this outer arch. The altar, as well as the east and north windows of the church, are Late Gothic. An old well near the doorway and a round tower to the northwest of the church complete the idyllic setting.

The visitor should also not neglect to see the remains of a Franciscan friary and the Dominican Black Friars Church, still in use, whose alabaster statue of the Trinity and sculpture of St. Dominic are well worth studying. As in Wexford, a bull ring and an ancient stone gate also suggest something of medieval life in Kilkenny.

Heading north to County Carlow one passes Dunmore Cave, where in 928, more than 1,000 people were massacred by the Vikings. In one of its chambers stands a large stalagmite known as the Market Cross.

Carlow

Carlow—Browne's Hill Dolmen

Carlow is essentially an industrial town, but an early-thirteenth-century Anglo-Norman castle makes a stop here worthwhile. It can be reached by going through a mineral-water bottling works, where one has to ask for the key to the fortress. The eastern half of the originally square structure and two round corner towers have survived repeated attacks. But even more interesting than this 700-year-old masonry is an ancient tomb site west of Carlow that is 4,000 years old, the Browne's Hill Dolmen (illus. 2, page 34). Its sloping capstone, weighing 100 tons, is probably the heaviest monolith of its kind, and it simply rests on its three supporting standing stones in the midst of cultivated fields. In Celtic times, dolmens were used by the Druids as sites for cult ceremonies and sacrifices. These fascinating, mysterious stones are mentioned in many of the sagas. Today, plowed furrows come up to within a few yards of the dolmen, and cows graze nearby. Yet one almost expects to be confronted suddenly by a figure from Irish legend—a fairy, perhaps, or a leprechaun. How was this stone moved here, and how was it set in place? These questions still have not been answered completely.

Carlow castle.

Laois

Timahoe—Dunamase

After a short side trip to see the well-preserved round tower—one of the largest in Ireland—and the church of *Timahoe*, with its beautiful Romanesque doorway, the next stop is not until beyond Stradbally, at the gloomy Norman castle of *Dunamase*, which stands atop the 200-foot Rock of Dunamase. Even in early Christian times, there was a primitive fortification on this strategic spot. At the time of the Anglo-Norman invasion, the castle belonged to the king of Leinster, Dermot MacMurrough, but after the marriage of his daughter Aoife (Eva) to Strongbow, it came into the hands of that Norman knight. In a sense the castle is a ruined, secular cashel (ring fort with stone rampart). The structure changed ownership a number of times, especially during the time of Cromwell, until in the late seventeenth century it was partially restored and made livable by Sir John Parnell. Later, it once again fell into disrepair.

The nearby village of Portlaoise offers little but a place to spend the night; in any case, Kildare and the horse country beckon.

Kildare

The Curragh—Kildare— Dún Ailinne—Old Kilcullen— Moone—Castledermot—Kilkea Castle

This area, in the heart of Ireland, is particularly captivating for horsemen and horse lovers. Known as *The Curragh*, its limestone soil is ideal for producing the best breeds, since it has a perfect hardness and produces good grass year round. Famed stud farms are hidden behind tall, green hedges; here, the magnificent Irish horses, whose most outstanding qualities are courage and strength, are trained. These horses are regulars at the racetrack, and they are also well known as fine trotters. Steeplechase riders commonly import these horses, and the breed is equally prized by polo players. But in addition to the Irish full-bloods, the area's Connemara horses, a gentle breed, are beloved worldwide.

One can watch the daily training of the racehorses, which takes place early in the morning. Their light, graceful gaits, their slender forms, and their glistening coats never fail to thrill, and anyone who has seen them break into a full gallop while the ground is still covered with dew can understand why so many Irish horses have become famous.

Hunting is almost more widespread in Ireland than in England. Roughly eighty packs of hounds are maintained on the island, many of them, such as the Kildare Hounds, in The Curragh. Whenever one of the hunting societies stages an early morning event, one can see members of the local gentry and nobility poised, waiting for the Master of Hounds. Then suddenly they are all racing off across hedges and meadows, streams and fences.

The Curragh also has golf courses, and since it is within easy reach of Dublin, it is a favorite district for outings and recreation. On race days as many as 100,000 people crowd into the grandstands of the largest racetracks, where horses from the National Stud meet their competition, and many

thousands of pounds change hands after each race.

The town of *Kildare* appears quite undisturbed by all this hubbub. It was here that St. Brigid, one of the great Irish saints, founded a monastery that housed both monks and nuns in the fifth or sixth century.

Kildare Cathedral, begun in the thirteenth century and expanded and restored in the fifteenth and nineteenth centuries, contains

RIGHT: Kildare Cathedral; FAR RIGHT: round tower and cross, Kildare.

94

a number of beautiful medieval tombs. Throughout the course of Irish church history, this cathedral has played an important role. Next to it, there is a round tower with a Romanesque portal and a conical roof.

Not far from the cathedral, there are a few foundation walls where St. Brigid's Firehouse stood. As a holdover from a pre-Christian sun cult, a perpetual fire was kept burning here, watched by St. Brigid and nineteen nuns. The poets honored St. Brigid as their patroness, celebrating her as "Mary of the Gaels, the Queen of the South." Today, St. Brigid's Day, celebrated on February 1, is one of the great Irish holidays. The people weave traditional, ancient sun symbols called Brigid's crosses, out of straw.

Instead of taking the road that leads directly toward Dublin, one can turn southward at Kilcullen. Soon, on the right, the silhouette of the hill fort *Dún Ailinne* comes into view. This fort, erected on the edge of

David with his harp, from the arm of the South Cross, Castledermot.

a hill, was the seat of the kings of Leinster for a time. Excavations have revealed that the spot has been inhabited since the Bronze Age. The circular wall, some 16 feet high and measuring roughly 50 yards in diameter, has an accompanying ditch—on the inside, surprisingly enough. The fort was lived in until the eighteenth century.

In the nearby precinct of *Old Kilcullen*, one discovers the fragment of a high cross that is decorated with figures on three sides. Those on the east side cannot be identified; they are possibly the apostles. The north side depicts David and the lion as well as a bishop; the west side, Samson and the lion. A number of intertwining ornaments decorate the south side. A round tower attests that there was once a monastic settlement here, and in fact it was founded by St. Patrick. St. Iserninus (died 469) was its first bishop, followed later by St. MacToil (died 548). Vikings attacked the house from nearby Dublin in the tenth century, and it was plundered in 932 and 944. A number of times, most recently in 1114, the whole settlement burned to the ground. What one sees today are the remains of a twelfth-century Romanesque stone church that was renovated in the eighteenth century. Farther south are the remains of a large motte

and bailey fort on the top of a hill near Ardscull.

Moone lies on the road leading from Old Kilcullen to Carlow. Here, as in Old Kilcullen, the granite high cross was the focal point of a Franciscan abbey. This early Bible cross has short arms, a small, narrow ring, and a slender base that continues upward to form the shaft (illus. 39, page 48). Its strikingly naïve low reliefs depict a number of familiar scenes:

East side: Daniel and seven lions (illus. 40, page 48), the sacrifice of Isaac, Adam and Eve, the Crucifixion

West side: the twelve apostles (illus. 38, p. 48), the Crucifixion, St. John

South side: the miracle of the loaves, the Flight into Egypt on the base, three youths in a fiery furnace along with various animals

North side: various figures and animals

Not far from this picturesquely situated cross is a well-preserved Early Romanes-

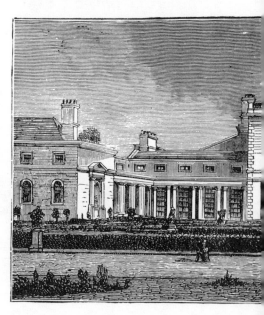

que church that probably belonged to the abbey founded by St. Columba.

A few miles farther to the south, in the center of *Castledermot*, an abbey founded by St. Dermot, there are two later crosses. Carved in granite, they represent a transitional stage between the ornamental cross and the Bible cross. Thanks to the enlarged and ornamented ends of the arms, a characteristic typical of Irish crosses, the cross ring seems thinner than, although not so graceful as, that of the Moone Cross. Favorite biblical motifs are depicted here as well. Rising from a base ornamented with a wave-like pattern, the shaft of the North Cross (illus. 37, page 47) is divided into three pictorial compartments and crowned by the representation in the cross's center. This cross depicts St. Anthony, Daniel in the lion's den, Adam and Eve, David with his harp (one of the few renderings of an Irish harp), and the sacrifice of Isaac. Its south side contains the miracle of the loaves. The scenes on the South Cross (illus. 36, page 47) are Christ's arrest, the Crucifixion, and, once again, Adam and Eve, David with his harp, and Daniel in the lion's den. On its base, one can make out various animals and human figures, possibly shepherds or hunters. A round tower constructed of irregular granite blocks, a reconstructed Romanesque doorway, and a number of early Christian and medieval gravestones form an appropriate setting for the two crosses in the verdant landscape.

Some 2.5 miles northwest of Castledermot is *Kilkea Castle*, which was once the seat of the Fitzgerald family. It was partially destroyed during a rebellion in 1798 but restored in the mid-nineteenth century. The well-preserved structure is now a hotel.

Carton House (built in 1740), near Maynooth, former seat of the Dukes of Leinster.

Wicklow

Baltinglass—Vale of Avoca —Piper's Stones—Glendalough —Laragh—Enniskerry— St. Valery's Cross

On the western slope of the wooded Wicklow Mountains lies the beautifully situated abbey of *Baltinglass*. Here again, one encounters the name of Dermot MacMurrough; he summoned a group of Cistercians from Mellifont to live in this new settlement in 1148. On the edge of a hill are the massive remains of the hill fort of Rathcoran and a prehistoric burial site. A passage grave with a short passageway and an ornamental stone sacrificial basin is surrounded by a double ring of stones. To the southwest of these stones is another passage grave, from the late Stone Age or early Iron Age, of which five depressions, the central chamber, and some spiral-ornamented stones are preserved. The site is encircled by an Iron Age defensive wall that was probably part of larger system of fortifications. It would thus appear that these all constitute the remains of a military and cultic center that evolved over a period of a thousand years.

The Christianized Irish commonly built their settlements in spots that had mythic or historical significance, and even the island's prehistoric inhabitants had a good eye for strategically favorable sites. For centuries, rebels withdrew to the high valleys of the Wicklow Mountains—hardly mountains in the American sense—which were within easy reach of Dublin. Their wooded summits and deep valleys support an almost Edenic vegetation, making the *Vale of Avoca* one of the favorite destinations of Dubliners and foreign visitors alike. Unfortunately, industrial complexes are multiplying in this district, which is the richest in ore in Ireland. It was here that gold was mined for centuries, even in pre-Christian times, and worked into a wide array of objects some of which one can now admire in the National Museum in Dublin.

The road to the northwest leads past the impressive *Piper's Stones*, a stone circle of uncertain date consisting of thirteen

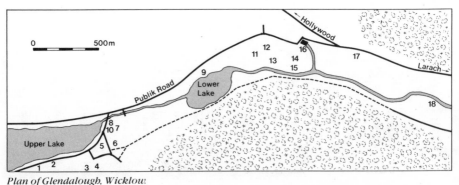

Plan of Glendalough, Wicklow.
1. Temple na Skellig; 2. St. Kevin's Bed; 3. St. Kevin's Cell; 4. Reefert Church; 5. Church site; 6–9. Crosses; 10. The Caher; 11. St. Mary's Church; 12. Round tower; 13. Priest's house; 14. Cathedral; 15. St. Kevin's Church; 16. Cross; 17. Trinity Church; 18. St. Saviour's Priory.

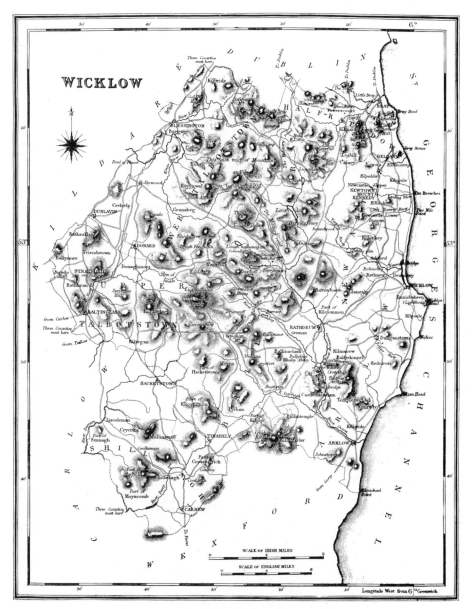

Map of Wicklow from Samuel Lewis's atlas, 1837.

granite monoliths, and on to a monastery founded by one of Ireland's greatest saints, the serene abbey of *Glendalough* (illus. 88 and 89, pages 187 and 188). According to legend, St. Kevin came to this high valley, hollowed out by glaciers and protected from the wind, and chose it as his "desert" in the sixth century. Here, beside the upper of two lakes dammed by glacial moraines, he was able to lead an ascetic life remote from the world. But slowly a small congregation began to gather around the saint, and over the next few centuries the settlement expanded farther down the valley until it became one of the largest religious communities, numbering several thousand monks and pupils. The Irish brothers generously provided education even for strangers, giving them free housing and placing books at their disposal. At that time the schooling of an educated person took scarcely less time than it does today. The sons of the upper classes had to attend school for up to eight years; if they hoped to be accepted into the community of scholars, twice that time was required. The course of study included not only subjects relating to the church, but also the scientific learning of the time.

Next to the Upper Lake, a small church, Temple na Skellig—unfortunately badly deteriorated—and a cave 3 feet high and 6 feet long that is known as St. Kevin's Bed constitute the remains of the saint's first settlement. It is likely that St. Kevin's Bed served as a shelter in the Bronze Age, long before the saint made his home in it. Both spots are easily reached only by boat.)

The "city" stands as the focal point of the monastery precinct, which stretches for 1.5 miles along the valley. The Seven Churches were constructed in later centuries; their remains, strewn about the valley, reveal early Irish Romanesque details. These small, rectangular churches are almost devoid of ornament. Like the few cells that have been preserved, they are purely functional. The ruins of a small beehive hut close to the Upper Lake are referred to as St. Kevin's Cell. Reefert Church and the various stone crosses seem less interesting than the buildings close to the road.

St. Mary's Church, from the tenth or eleventh century, reveals a few Romanesque embellishments in its east window and west portal. A well-preserved round tower with a new conical roof looms over the remains

St. Kevin's Bed.

Round tower and stone cross, Glendalough.

of the venerable cathedral, the main church at Glendalough. The walls of the cathedral, which was once the center of the religious life of the community, now support only a few medieval grave slabs. The oldest part of the church was its nave, from the eleventh century, to which the chancel and a sacristy were added in the twelfth century. Like the cathedral, the nearby Priest's House boasts a twelfth-century Romanesque door-

St. Kevin's Church.

way. But the major attraction of the Priest's House is a finely worked relief, of which a portion is sadly missing. A seated central figure is flanked in this gable sculpture by two kneeling figures, one of whom is carrying a staff.

St. Kevin's Church, also known as St. Kevin's Kitchen, is the only church at Glendalough that is completely preserved. The steep roof of this chapel built of mica-slate leaves room for a small attic above the nave. Its modest proportions, as well as the slant of the gables toward the inside, reveal how much this eleventh- or twelfth-century structure owes to the tradition of early Christian churches, even though the small bell tower on its roof appears to be unique (illus. 89, page 188). A high cross of the twelfth-century type is preserved in the nave of the small chapel, along with fragments from the other churches. This cross possibly once stood along the pilgrim's road to Glendalough. Its figural decoration consists only of a depiction of the Crucifixion in the center of the short-armed cross. The saint represented on the shaft may be St. Kevin. Intertwining ornaments embellish the back.

St. Kieran's Church and Trinity Church, though interesting, are not essential to see, but St. Saviour's Priory must not be missed. Standing 1 mile down the valley, this youngest church of the settlement is by no means the least important. St. Laurence O'Toole, who was once the abbot of Glendalough and later the bishop of Dublin, founded this church in 1162 or possibly a bit earlier. (St. Laurence O'Toole is the only canonized Irish saint. All the others, St. Patrick, St. Columba, and St. Brigid, are not officially recognized as saints in Rome.) The chancel arch and particularly the east window contain numerous geometric and animal motifs as well as human faces. The later ad-

St. Saviour's Priory.

ditions to St. Saviour's lead up to its second story, above the chancel. Photographers can shoot splendid contrast pictures here in the morning light.

The road now leads down through rolling hills with oak forests to *Laragh*, which lies at the head of two glens, Glenmacnass and Glendasan. The seclusion and tranquility of this area make it well worth visiting. It is overgrown with oaks, beeches, and holly, and one can also find exotic subtropical vegetation here. But Dublin awaits, as one leaves the granite Wicklow Mountains behind and drives northward toward *Enniskerry*. Powerscourt House, the seat of the Powerscourt family, was designed by Richard Cassels in the best English stucco country-house style. It is not open to visitors, but it is the extraordinary park, perhaps the loveliest in Ireland, that truly attracts the visitor. Powerscourt Park represents the quintessential English cultivated landscape, and it also offers a splendid view of the Wicklow Mountains. An hour's stroll along idyllic paths beside the Dargle River, past eucalyptus and other exotic trees, brings one to the tallest waterfall in Ireland, nearly 330 feet high.

St. Valery's Cross (illus. 59, page 121) near Fassaroe, is the last stop before Dublin. This late cross from the twelfth century boasts a ring that is not pierced but is ornamented with a Crucifixion scene. The form of this cross can be seen nowhere else.

Dublin

Christ Church Cathedral— St. Patrick's Cathedral— St. Werburgh's Church—Dublin Castle—Trinity College— National Museum—National Gallery—Howth

The city of Dublin in the county of the same name, is the political and cultural center of Ireland. Ptolemy's world map from the second century A.D. shows only a minor military settlement on the banks of the Liffey, and the town grew very little larger in early Christian times. The royal residence remained at Tara, somewhat farther to the north. Only after the Vikings had built up a settlement at the river ford in the ninth century—and changed the town's name from the old Celtic *Baile Átha Cliath* (Gaelic for "place near the ford") to *Dubh Linn* (Gaelic for "black swamp")—did Dublin begin to develop into the important city that it is today. Although there are now more snack bars and Chinese and Indian restaurants than native pubs, Dublin has a distinct charm of its own: in part a miniature London, in part an Irish town. For centuries, the city was influenced by English culture, and it has adopted many English qualities. Therefore the Irish love Dublin, but they do not consider it to be typically their own. Dubliners, however, are proud of the city's history and its literary past, which includes Swift, Yeats, Shaw, and Joyce, and also recall its contributions to music, such as the premiere performance of Handel's *Messiah*. Dublin alone would be worthy of a separate volume. Here though, only the most important buildings and the monuments of Irish art can be dealt with.

Christ Church Cathedral

Christ Church of the Holy Trinity, as it is called in full, has long been the center of religious life in Ireland; the first archbish-

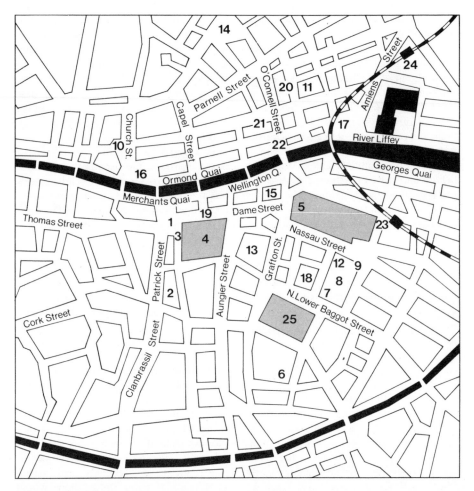

Downtown Dublin.
1. Christ Church Cathedral; 2. St. Patrick's Cathedral; 3. St. Werburgh's Cathedral; 4. Dublin Castle; 5. Trinity College and College Park; 6. University College; 7. National Museum; 8. Leinster House; 9. National Gallery; 10. St. Michan's Church; 11. St. Mary's Cathedral; 12. National Library; 13. Municipal Museum; 14. Municipal Gallery of Modern Art; 15. Old Parliament House; 16. Four Courts; 17. Custom House; 18. Mansion House; 19. City Hall; 20. Irish Tourist Office; 21. Main Post Office; 22. O'Connell Bridge; 23. Pearse Station; 24. Amiens Street Station; 25. St. Stephen's Green.

ops were consecrated and buried here, and all important occasions were celebrated in the church. Its dark, gloomy appearance, its wonderful calm, and the tomblike atmosphere that its funeral monuments evoke give it a special character.

Dunan, the first bishop of Dublin, founded the first church on this site in about 1038. The land was provided by King Sitric of Dublin. Until the Irish church became independent in 1152, Christ Church was subordinate to Canterbury Cathedral in England. An attack by the Anglo-Normans demolished the original structure. Shortly afterward, the Irish archbishop Laurence O'Toole substituted for the secular clergy a community of Augustinian canons, and the cloister church became the main church of the order. In about 1170, work began on the church one sees today (illus. 130, page 240). The oldest portions are the crypt and the Romanesque portal on the south transept. The crypt, the only one in Ireland that runs the full length of the nave, contains a number of architectural remnants from older portions of the church, and statues of the last Stuart kings of England, Charles II and James II, have also been set up here. Members of the underground Irish Republican

Army (IRA) blew up the monument to their symbolic archenemy, William of Orange.

The layout of the cathedral shows an English influence. Portions of the north and south transepts may survive from the first church. In the twelfth century, windows in the Early Gothic style were added. The present nave, from about 1212, is ascribed to John Comyn, who was archbishop then; its western end was completed about twenty years later. The choir, which was expanded in the fourteenth century, the north side of the nave, and the twoer date from the period of the Early English style—circa 1230.

Like all churches in the English style, Christ Church contains many tombs. Tradition has it that the monument topped by a knight in armor on the south side of the nave is the last resting place of Strongbow. And the small sarcophagus next to it is said to contain the remains of his son, whom he struck in two with his sword for cowardice in the face of the enemy. But the grave dates from the year 1340 and thus is much too late. It is of course possible that the two sarcophagi merely mark the spot where Strongbow and his son were buried originally. It is certain that the woman portrayed in the Chapel of St. Laurence

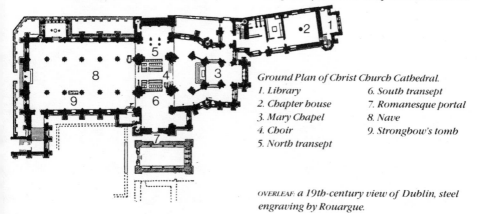

Ground Plan of Christ Church Cathedral.

1. Library
2. Chapter house
3. Mary Chapel
4. Choir
5. North transept
6. South transept
7. Romanesque portal
8. Nave
9. Strongbow's tomb

OVERLEAF: a 19th-century view of Dublin, steel engraving by Rouargue.

A 19th-century view of St. Patrick's Cathedral.

Ground plan of St. Patrick's Cathedral.
1. *Mary Chapel*
2. *Choir*
3. *North transept*
4. *South transept*
5. *Nave*
6. *Tower*
7. *Guiness Monument*

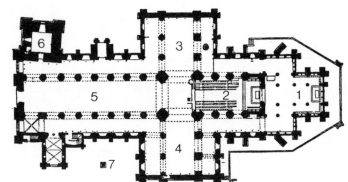

O'Toole is Aoifes (Eva), Dermot MacMurrough's daughter and Strongbow's wife. Countless other well-preserved gravestones, among them that of a bishop from the twelfth or thirteenth century, ornament the walls and the floor of the church.

The Augustinian chapter house, erected in the thirteenth century, once stood to the south of the church. A Romanesque arch of the church towers over its remains. In about 1541, the priory was turned into an Anglican chapel, and its greatest treasure, the staff of St. Patrick, was destroyed while the church was being plundered.

St. Patrick's Cathedral

St. Patrick's Cathedral (illus. 126, page 239), the younger of the two Dublin cathedrals, has suffered from plundering and fires just as Christ Church has. But after extensive renovations, it has regained its place as one of the most important sacred structures. According to tradition, St. Patrick baptized converts at a well on the site of the present-day cathedral, and it is also possible that a pre-Norman church once stood here. St. Patrick's was raised to the status of a cathedral in 1213; at that time, the Lady Chapel opening off the east side of the choir was constructed. In 1316, the church went up in flames when the Scot Edward Bruce and his army stormed Dublin. After the fire, Archbishop Thomas Minot rebuilt the north tower and large portions of the north aisle.

St. Patrick's and Christ Church have each functioned as the leading Irish church a number of times. The cathedral's connection to Irish literature and culture is attested by a number of imposing tombs and inscriptions. Foremost among them is the grave of one of the great names in world literature —Jonathan Swift. Not only did he write immortal satires, but he also was dean of the cathedral (1713–1745). This brilliant rebel attacked the faults and shortcomings of his contemporaries in his works such as *Gulliver's Travels*, and fought with all the means available to him against tyranny. He continues to pose a number of riddles to historians. The complex story of his love affairs with Esther Johnson (Stella), the woman who is buried beside him, and with Esther Vantomrigh (Vanessa) will probably never be untangled. Only after he had ensured his career in London did he settle in Dublin, where he became involved in political intrigues. Indeed, Dublin is so indebted to him that John Keats wrote, "He is always around the next corner."

Swift was especially fond of the biting form of Irish humor that still survives. He willed that on his death his estate be used for the construction of a mental institution, St. Patrick's Hospital. The epitaph Swift wrote for himself reveals his rebellious spirit, and contains more wisdom than might be apparent on first reading:

Hic depositum est Corpus
Jonathan Swift, S.T.D.
Huius Ecclesiae Cathedralis
Decanus
Ubi Saeva indignatio
Ulterius
Ea lacerare nequit.
Abi, viator,
Et imitare, si poteris,
Strenuum pro virili
Libertatis vindicatorem.
Obiit 19° de mensis Octobris
A.D. 1745, Anno Aetatis 78.

[Here lies the body of Jonathan Swift, doctor of theology, dean of this cathedral, where wild indignation can no longer tear at his heart. Go, pilgrim, and bear yourself, as best you can, like the eternal champion of liberty. He died on the 19th of the month of October in the year 1745 A.D. at the age of 78.]

The spongy ground on which the cathedral is built, lying between two courses of the Poddle River, not only made the construction of a crypt impossible. but also has caused a number of the bones of those buried there to be flooded away.

The last Irish bard, Turlough O'Carolan (1670–1738), is also commemorated in St. Patrick's. A plaque in a corner of the north tower recalls this tradition that stayed alive much longer in Ireland than in the other Celtic lands. The banners hanging in the church honor the Order of St. Patrick, which was founded by George III. In the south transept, there is a door through which, in 1491, the earls of Ormonde and of Kildare shook hands, ending years of bloody feuding. Outside, on the south side of the church, stands the monument to Sir Benjamin Guinness, who donated £150,000 toward the renovation of the structure in the nineteenth century.

St. Werburgh's Church and Dublin Castle

Not far from St. Patrick's, one comes via Bridge Street to the small *St. Werburgh's Church*, a neo-Classical structure on the site of an early Christian foundation ascribed to St. Martin of Tours. Later, in the twelfth century, a Nordic church, the original St. Werburgh's, was built here. The most interesting monument in the church is the medieval tomb of a famous revolutionary, Lord Edward Fitzgerald of the Purcel clan, who was betrayed and executed in 1798.

From St. Werburgh's Church, a right turn at the next corner brings one face to face with a mixture of all of the styles from the Middle Ages to the Tudor period. This is *Dublin Castle*, long the seat of temporal authority, where the respective viceroys attempted to carry out the directives of their rulers more or less faithfully. It is the history of the structure itself, however, that draws one to it. A tour of St. Patrick's Hall, the throne room, and the neo-Gothic chapel summons up a picture of English might. The Genealogical Office in the castle can provide a family tree for anyone of Irish descent.

Trinity College

The existing buildings of *Trinity College*, which Catholics were long forbidden to enter, were built between 1755 and 1759 by the architects Henry Keane and John Sanderson (illus. 128, page 239). Elizabeth I founded the university for about 70 students in 1591, but no structures from that time have been preserved. The first female student was admitted in 1903. Today, the college houses more than 2,500 students.

The first quadrangle, known as Parliament Square and built in the eighteenth century, lies directly behind the entrance gate which is flanked by statues of Goldsmith and Burke. But the visitor is most likely to head directly for the Old Library, which is in the second quadrangle and which also dates from the eighteenth century. It houses nearly 1 million printed books, 5,000 manuscripts, and world-famous codices that make it a major scholarly center. A broad staircase leads up to the dark, wood-paneled Long Room, where exhibitions are held and manuscripts are displayed. The Book of Kells lies in several glass cases (illus. 26 and 27, pages 42 and 43). The metal casket in which it was preserved, known as the Cumdach, has been missing since the plundering of the cloister, when the last abbot, Plunkett, placed the volume in the hands of Archbishop Henry Ussher, one of the founders of Trinity

Trinity College Library.

Bell Tower, Trinity College.

College. The 340 pages of the manuscript, all but two of which are illuminated, were bound into four volumes in 1953. Other noteworthy volumes here are the Book of Durrow from the seventh century, whose silver case is also long since lost; the eighth-century Book of Dimma; and the ninth-century Book of Armagh. These last two lie in a beautiful case of a later date. The surrounding cases contain manuscripts of Milton and the Irish writers Goldsmith, Swift, Yeats, and Wilde, as well as letters of Mary, Queen of Scots.

In a case at the end of the Long Room, the oldest-known Irish harp is displayed. The instrument is considerably smaller than today's concert harp, which dates only from the Baroque period, because it had to be easily transported; its base is also more compact. This harp is said to have belonged to the legendary Brian Ború (died 1014), who fell in the Battle of Clontarf, but it is most probably not more than 600 years old.

Other Irish manuscripts, such as the Book of Ballymotte and the Book of Ui Maine, are exhibited in Dublin's University College.

National Museum

The *National Museum*, together with Leinster House and the National Gallery, forms an impressive complex in the monumental English style of the past few centuries. It preserves artistic treasures of all periods, and a stroll through its galleries is an unforgettable experience.

The large gallery houses works of art that were for the most part acquired from the Royal Irish Academy in 1891. The most important grouping consists of the cases in the center. Most notable of all is the Tara Brooch (illus. 20 and 21, page 41), which was discovered in 1850 near Bettystown (and has no connection to Tara, the seat of the Irish kings). It represents the most exquisite example of the art of Irish goldsmiths. Enameling had been fully developed by the eighth century, when the Tara Brooch

41. Muiredach Cross, probably the most richly ornamented high cross in Ireland. Early 10th century. Height: 17 feet, 7 inches, Monasterboice, Louth.

42. Muiredach Cross, depiction of the Crucifixion at the intersection of the arms, Monasterboice.

43. East Cross and round tower, Monasterboice. ▷

44. Muiredach Cross, Adam and Eve, Cain and Abel, Monasterboice.

45. Muiredach Cross, Christ's arrest, Monasterboice.

46. North Cross, east face, 10th century, Duleek, Mea[th]

47. South Cross, west face, 9th century, Kells, Meath.

48. Market Cross, 9th century, Kells.

49. Fragmentary high cross and round tower, Kells.

50. East Cross, 10th century, Durrow, Offaly.

51. South Cross, 9th century, Clonmacnoise, Offaly.

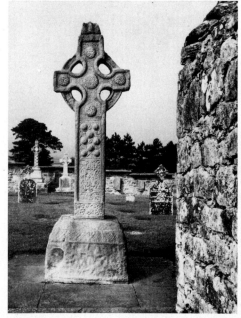

52. High crosses and small round tower, Clonmacnoise.

53. Clonmacnoise—view toward the Shannon.

54. West (Inscription) Cross, Clonmacnoise.

55. High cross, 11th century, Drumcliff, Sligo.

56, 57. Late cross (12th century) with large-figure depiction of a crucifixion and a bishop. Height: 12 feet, 7 inches; ornamented face of the cross, Dysert O'Dea, Clare.

58. Doorty Cross, 12th century. Ornamented side with highly simplified figural depictions, Kilfenora, Clare.

59. St. Valery's Cross, 12th century. The ring and the arms form a single unit, near Fassaroe, Wicklow.

60, 61. Farmhouse and herd of sheep, Connemara, Galway.

62. Dongory Castle, near Kinvara, Galway.

63. Upper Lough Leane, Kerry.

64, 65. Grianán of Aileach, one of the most important ring forts, lies on a hill in Donegal, west of Londonderry (Northern Ireland).

66. Dún Aengus, one of the most massive prehistoric fortified sites in Europe, on Inishmore, Galway.

67. Staigue Fort, a ring layout (diameter: 98 feet) on the south coast of the Iveragh Peninsula, Kerry.

68. The glen of Aherlow, Tipperary. ▷

69. St. Columba's House, Kells, Meath.

70. Beehive hut, near Slea Head, Kerry.

71. The boat-shaped Gallarus Oratory, 8th century, on the Dingle Peninsula, Kerry.

was made. At that time, jewelers worked in gilt bronze, inlaid designs of silver and copper, *millefiori*, and yellow enamel. They also set twisted glass rods in silver and created works with wavelike silver threads and green, yellow, or red enamel. The Tara Brooch is relatively small, not quite 4 inches long, and yet it combines most of these techniques in a splendid degree of refinement.

The outer embossed verge and the large V-shaped end of the pin culminate in the heads of serpents and birds. The heavy circle frames a number of compartments filled with exquisite animals in gold filigree, with woven golden wire, key designs, and flanges for amber inlays. Large blue and red bosses interrupt the arrangement. There is a profusion of minute, delicate embellishment, covering the surfaces of the back of the head of the pin and the circle, on which elongated compartments filled with trumpet spirals alternate with interwoven and cross-hatched bands of animals and birds. The depressions in the trumpet spirals on the back of the end part are filled with niello, a blackish alloy most uncommon in Irish art of that time. (Máire and Liam de Paor, *Old Ireland*, p. 132)

Celtic love of illustration and medieval sobriety of form combine in a number of superb creations on display here. Several reliquaries reflect the country's reverence for its saints and the founders of its monasteries. One example is the bronze Belt Reliquary of Moylough, which was discovered in a bog near Sligo. The use of both red and yellow enamel, novel at that time, forced the artist to simplify his lines and clearly separate the individual fields with bronze flanges. Enamel, often in combination with *millefiori* glass, was then applied in L- and T-shaped panels. Silver bosses provide contrast on this unusual reliquary.

Exhibited nearby are several Ogham stones, with inscriptions generally limited to a name (though sometimes including the person's father as well), which suggests that they were intended as grave markers. (illus. 18, page 40).

The glass cases in the center house a wealth of early objects, chiefly from the Bronze Age. Simple garment fasteners, as well as the sickle-shaped, hammered gold lunules worn as necklaces and collar rings, amply testify to Ireland's role as one of the ancient world's great gold producers. The Feakle Treasure, which was discovered in Clare in 1948, is the first major Bronze Age find; dated to 650 B.C., the treasure consists of a gorget and other ornaments.

The prize of the collection, discovered together with an unornamented chalice and several brooches in Ardagh (Limerick) in 1868, is the massive silver Ardagh Chalice (illus. 22 and 23, pages 41 and 42). By Celtic standards its ornamentation is quite restrained, which suggests possible Continental influences. The Irish art historians and archeologists Máire and Liam de Paor describe the chalice as follows:

Spiral ornament from the Belt Reliquary of Moylough.

129

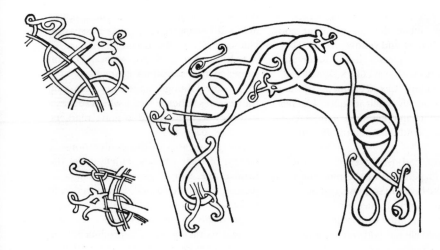

Details from the Clonmacnoise crosier. RIGHT: *crosier of the abbots of Clonmacnoise.*

The embellishments in gold, gilt bronze, glass, and enamel are found on the handles, a band below the lip of the chalice, on the four separate plaquettes on its bowl, on the throat, and on the band encircling the flat portion of the foot. The filigree of the main ornamental band below the rim is particularly exquisite, of almost microscopic fineness. It is built up of beaded or woven gold wires that are soldered onto a gold ground into which the outlines of the designs had first been impressed. The bosses and some of the angular enamel plates appear to be subdivided by steplike or straight lattices. In fact these are fine silver grids set into the surface of the enamel; often red enamel has also been fitted into the outside of the blue glass. Several of the bosses have small circular centerpieces of granulated gold, and in certain spots on the handles granulation appears on two levels: on the tiny raised sections and on the background as well. Small

circles have been chased in the swelling borders of the main ornamental band so as to attain a stronger contrast against the smooth silver surface of the chalice itself. Below this band the names of the twelve apostles in the elegant script of the Lindisfarne Gospels are contained in a strip dulled by chasing. A notched ornament of remarkable precision graces the throat, and on the band below it there are compartments filled with fine sliver tracery, each with a different design. Other compartments have small inlays of light blue glass, through which one can faintly discern the chased design on the gold behind them. (*Old Ireland*, p. 133)

A separate display consists of the bishop's crosiers of St. Berach, St. Mura of Fahan, and St. Dymphna of Tedavnet, all from the eleventh century, their crooks set on ordinary wooden staffs. Scandinavian designs in the Ringerike–Urnes style ornament the staff

Ringerike pattern from the Kells crosier.

of the abbots of Clonmacnoise, and the animal head at the start of its curve recalls Scandinavian carving.

The Kells crosier, from the tenth century, boasts pierced bird forms in the Celtic ornamental style. The designs of the neck grip are in the Ringerike style that became typical of the eleventh century; they reveal individual, stylized leaf forms with acanthus motifs, executed in intricate silver tracery and niello. Soon the Irish goldsmiths would replace such leaf motifs with traditional animal embellishments, as in the book reliquaries of the *Cathach* and the Misach from Kells.

St. Patrick's Bell Casket, from the twelfth century, is of cast bronze ornamented in the Scandinavian Urnes style. Its central motif of grapevines with birds is much less common in Irish than in Continental art. This casket was created to house the Bell of St. Patrick, the oldest-known surviving piece of Irish metalwork (c. 406). Another beautiful work is the Clogán Oir, the Golden Bell of St. Senan. Shortly after the turn

Animal patterns from the Kells crosier.

of the eleventh century, after the Irish victory under Brian Ború, the art of goldsmithing took on a renewed importance, as proved by numerous caskets, reliquaries, and crosses from this period.

Soiscel Molaise, the first of three book reliquaries, resembles the eleventh-century Drumcliff Cross in its ornamentation. The depiction of human figures comes to the fore, as the relief of the saint entwined in animal ornaments attests. The small animal embellishments, somewhat influenced by Scandinavian styles, were the favored decoration of this period. The second, the Stowe Missal, created between 1045 and 1052, reveals several animal scenes, such as a pack of dogs on a deer hunt, that are set apart from the general ornamentation. Here, as in the third, the Breac Maodhóg Reliquary, the Irish Romanesque style has asserted it-

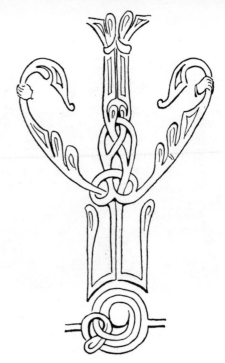

Foliage pattern from the Breac Maodhóg Reliquary.

self over Scandinavian forms. On the Breac Maodhóg, fashioned in the eleventh century for St. Maodhóg of Drumlane (Cavan), one marvels at the precise rendition of the garments and its intricate designs.

Three additional pieces deserve attention. The engraved Arm Reliquary of St. Lachtin from the south of Ireland shows twelfth-century variants of the Irish Romanesque style. The enamels are red, yellow, and white, and some of its checkered designs achieve the effect of *millefiori* glass.

The most beautiful work of Irish art in the Urnes style, the Processional Cross of Cong, was a reliquary for a splinter of the True Cross. It was created by goldsmiths in 1123 at the command of Turlough O'Connor for the church at Tuam. The basic materials in the 29-inch cross are riveted gilt bronze plates.

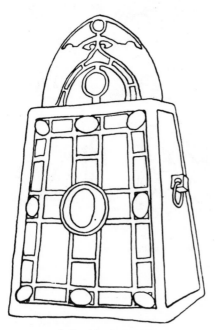

St. Patrick's Bell Casket.

Below the shaft of the large Latin cross itself there is first a round base, the upper part of which is in the form of a large, cast animal head that holds the shaft of the cross in his mouth. Along the edge of the shaft and the crossbeam there protrude at intervals the settings for enamels. Red enamel in cruciform shapes and steplike patterns has been inlaid, as on the Ardagh Chalice, into yellow. On the back side four bars have been covered for their entire length up to the point where they meet with pierced and gilt fields of cast bronze in front of the plain bronze background of the inner casing. This piercework forms a fine mesh of animal forms that are almost symmetrically arranged on either side of the central axis. (Máire and Liam de Paor, *Old Ireland*, p. 187)

On the Cross of Cong, it is possible to see the favorite motifs of the Urnes style quite clearly. Animal bodies in the form of broad bands and with long, pointed heads cover the shaft of the cross, often twisting themselves into the shape of a figure eight. This motif persisted much longer in Ireland than did the acanthus leaf pattern because it was more readily adapted to traditional Celtic animal ornamentation. Only on the large head that bites into the shaft can one see small leaf designs like those on the Reliquary of St. Manchan.

The coming church reform and the collapse of the power of the monasteries brought an end to such traditional handicraft —and to its monastic patrons. The house-shaped Reliquary of St. Manchan is therefore the last interesting piece one sees here. Animal ornaments similar to those on the Cross

Figures from St. Manchan's shrine.

A 19th-century view of Howth Harbor.

of Cong are more confusing and less unified in their effect; a decline can already be perceived. Soon there was no longer a demand for work of this kind, and the fall of monastic culture sealed the fate of the goldsmith's art. Henceforth, metalwork for the church was mass-produced by shops.

Unless one is interested in the symbols of English domination—uniforms, armor, and so on—one can leave this museum and proceed past Leinster House, the Irish Parliament, to the National Gallery of Ireland.

National Gallery

Ireland came into contact with classical painting only by way of England and has produced nothing uniquely its own in this art form. Nevertheless, the *National Gallery*, where Handel's *Messiah* was first performed, contains much that is worth seeing.

The first rooms of the gallery are given over to portraits. Here one finds William Butler Yeats as portrayed by his brother John Butler Yeats, and likenesses of Shaw, Joyce, Swift and his Stella, Burke, and many other literary and historical personages. The Spanish room boasts Goya's *A Spanish Woman* and El Greco's *St. Francis*. The next three rooms are dedicated to Dutch masters, including Rembrandt's *Flight into Egypt* (1647) and *Head of an Old Man* (c. 1650) as well as works by Huysum, Ruisdael, Hals, and Van de Velde. The Irish paintings from the nineteenth century in the following rooms are less significant. Upstairs one comes upon works of the Italian school: Fra Angelico, Uccello, Bellini, Signorelli, Ghirlandaio, Giorgione, Coreggio, Tintoretto, Veronese, Canaletto, Guardi, and Bellotto. Following these are representative works, if not always of top quality, by Rubens, Van Dyck, Brueghel, Dirk Bouts, and Cranach; Gainsborough, Turner, Constable, and Hogarth; and Corot, Millet, Géricault, Delacroix, Monet, and Degas.

Dublin can also satisfy a number of other

interests. The Dublin Horse Show, for example, which is held every summer, attracts horse lovers and trainers from all over the world. Among the city's favorite diversions are dog racing, Gaelic football, and hurling, an old Irish game similar to modern-day field hockey. At times, one can almost sense the atmosphere that suffuses the works of the great writers. The dreary, often melancholy air of the older, poorer districts combines with the noises of a first Anglicized, then Americanized, big city.

Howth

To the northeast of Dublin, the Howth Peninsula reaches far out into the sea. From it one has a splendid panorama of the city and its harbor. In *Howth* is the particularly remarkable St. Mary's Church, a foundation from the eleventh century that contains a beautiful tomb in its south aisle. This tomb of St. Laurence O'Toole is ornamented with stone reliefs of a Crucifixion scene and depictions of St. Michael and two angels. Its east side is graced by figures of St. Thomas of Canterbury, St. Peter, and St. Katherine of Alexandria, true masterworks from about 1470. Howth has often played an important role in the defense of Dublin. The Anglo-Normans first landed on its beach, as did the armies of Cromwell centuries later.

Passing Dublin's airport at Collinstown and the town of Swords, with its thirteenth-century castle, one follows the main road to the north. After the fishing village of Balbriggan, one passes along the short coastline of Meath and into Louth, the smallest county in Ireland.

Louth

Drogheda—Monasterboice—Mellifont—Proleek Dolmen

Drogheda, like Dublin and Wexford, is one of the settlements along the east coast that were conquered or founded by the Vikings. Its *St. Laurence Gate* (illus. 78, page 181) towers over the narrow streets and poorhouses of the town, which was founded in 901. No other structure in Ireland provides such an impressive picture of the massive Viking style, with the possible exception of the Reginald Tower in Waterford. The dimensions of the barbican give a clear idea of the strength of the whole fortification. In the Middle Ages, Drogheda was the site of countless parliaments and rivaled cities like Dublin and Cork, until Cromwell's butchery put an end to its power in 1649. From Drogheda, one can proceed to the important monastic settlements of Monasterboice and Mellifont.

Monasterboice was founded by St. Buithe, who first traveled through Italy, Germany, and England before settling here. There are many unbelievable legends about this saint. It is said that on his travels he cured the sick; once, like a second Moses, he is supposed to have parted the waters of the Boyne. He even brought back to life a man who had been decapitated. It is possible that in his youth St. Buithe came to know St. Patrick. When he died in 521, he foretold the coming of St. Columba, who allegedly was born at that very moment. His monastery differs little from early Christian communities already described. And like most of them, it was not spared plundering by the Vikings. But Domhnall, the high king of Tara, was able to liberate it from their domination in 968.

The chief attractions of Monasterboice today are its Bible crosses, notably the 17-foot Muiredach Cross (illus. 41, page

*East and west sides of the Muire-
dach Cross, Monasterboice.*

113). Standing not far from the entrance, it is the most richly ornamented example of its type. The inscription on its base, which asks for a prayer for the abbot Muiredach, has given the cross its name, although it should not be thought of as a grave cross. It is quite certain that Muiredach (died 922) is the person referred to, and accordingly the cross can be dated to the beginning of the tenth century, the "baroque" period of early Irish sculpture. Its ornamentation served primarily as a picture Bible for the faithful.

East side: The first compartment represents the Fall and the murder of Abel by Cain (illus 44, page 116). Above it are David and Goliath. In the third scene, Moses is striking water from the rock, and the fourth shows the Adoration of the Magi. This chronological sequence culminates in a dynamic depiction of the Last Judgment. In the cen-

ter is the crucified Christ. Below the figure of Christ, the archangel Michael is weighing souls, while David plays an Irish harp to the left. Above this scene, the Holy Ghost is depicted in the form of a bird. The top of the cross is formed by a casketlike crest on which St. Paul and St. Anthony are pictured in the desert. The ornamented stone ring supports cross arms that are wider at their ends, as is typically Irish.

West side: This face appears to be less forceful than the east side. Two reclining lions ornament the aforementioned inscription on the base. Above it, in the first compartment, Christ is being arrested by two officers armed with swords (illus. 45, page 116). This relief gives an especially good picture of the typical clothing of the tenth century. The scenes above this may depict the doubting Thomas and Christ with Peter and Paul. A number of unidentified saints

Ruins at Monasterboice.

St. Lawrence Gate, Drogheda.

surround the Crucifixion scene in the center (illus. 42, page 114), above which Moses and Aaron are praying. Another possible but less likely interpretation of this scene is that it represents the confrontation between the abbot Muiredach and Viking warriors from nearby Annagassan, showing their conversion, tonsure, and dismissal.

North side: This side is covered with various ornaments that are interrupted only by a chiseled hand of God just below the arm of the cross and reliefs of St. Paul and St. Anthony.

South side: This side portrays the Flight into Egypt and Pilate washing his hands, along with numerous ornaments, among which are grapevines and leaves. The base is covered with pictures of hunters, animals, and fabulous creatures.

Close to the tower stands the West Cross from the same period. Its ornamentation is more obscure.

East side: Here, David is killing a lion and Abraham prepares to sacrifice Isaac. Beneath the arrest of Christ, the three youths are sitting in the fiery furnace. In the center is the uncommon motif of the Ascension. Above these, St. Michael is battling with Satan.

West side: Soldiers guard Christ's tomb, and it is also possible to make out the baptism of Christ and the kiss of Judas. The remaining scenes are so weathered that they cannot be identified.

The five-story round tower was destroyed in 1097 by a fire that raged while the monks struggled to rescue their library and other treasures. It has been restored, however, and today it is possible to climb its iron ladders all the way to the top. Through a window, one steps out onto a small viewing platform from which the whole area can be surveyed. In good weather, it is even possible to see the coast from here. (The key can be obtained in the gift shop next to the parking area.)

A few miles from Monasterboice, there is a site that presents a picture of a totally different kind of cloister: Mellifont, the first Cistercian monastery on Irish soil (illus. 80 and 81, pages 181 and 182). While Monasterboice belonged to an independent early church that considered itself only partially subject to Rome, Mellifont was a foundation of a powerful order that sought— with the support of the clergy at Canterbury, strong allies of the pope—to regenerate the Irish populace after the unrest and confusion of the eleventh century. Comparison of the architecture of the two establishments reveals a stark contrast. Monasterboice is an early fortress cloister with small, keel-shaped churches and beehive monks' cells, while the Early Gothic structures of Mellifont are based on Continental models.

Mellifont was founded in response to a request by St. Malachy|O'Morgair, the bishop of Armagh. A group of French monks was dispatched to establish the abbey by St. Bernard of Clairvaux, the renovator of the Cistercian order. The idyllic land on which it stands—and from which it took its name (Latin for "honey spring")—was donated to the brothers by Donnchad O'Ceorbhaill, the king of Oriel. Construction took fifteen years, and the abbey was consecrated in 1157. The ceremony was attended by the papal legate, the high king Murtough O'Loughlim, his nobles, other personages of rank, and crowds of commoners.

Mellifont suffered the fate of most monasteries. After it was overrun by Henry VIII's troops in 1539 and Cromwell's in 1649, only the foundation walls of the church remained. One can easily reconstruct the architecture, however, because of its similarity to Continental structures. A partially preserved, two-story, octagonal lavabo (washhouse), unique in Ireland, is its most striking feature. This spot is so tranquil today that one may forget that it was an extremely dynamic spiritual center and seat of learning.

In addition to Monasterboice and Mellifont, Louth offers the great dolmen of *Proleek*, but it requires a rather extended side trip to the north. Certainly anyone who does not visit Browne's Hill should have a look at this splendid example. The dolmen lies northwest of Dundalk on the grounds of the Ballymascanlan Hotel. Its capstone weighs roughly 40 tons. (Drive onto the grounds of the hotel; just before the main building, a little bridge leads from the parking lot to the outbuildings. After passing between the buildings, turn left at the fork in the maintenance road. A little over 100 yards beyond the fork there is a gate, and from here it is necessary to hike about half a mile to reach the dolmen, following a path across the fields. A few yards in front of the dolmen are the remains of a wedge-shaped gallery grave.)

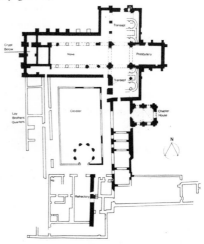

Ground plan of Mellifont Abbey.

Meath

Slane—Newgrange—Dowth—Knowth—Duleek—Tara—Trim—Bective Abbey—Kells—Loughcrew

County Meath is probably the richest district in Ireland in terms of historical and artistic monuments. Since the very earliest times, Meath has been the heartland of the island. The tourist who is on a tight schedule and wishes to get out of Dublin for a day or two and experience something of the "real" Ireland will find everything here: ancient barrow graves, tranquil abbeys, and massive Norman gates. The Boyne flows picturesquely and calmly through the garden-like landscape, past royal seats and high crosses, until it reaches the sea at Drogheda.

An important stop in Meath is the hill of *Slane*, where St. Patrick is said to have lighted the first Easter fire in Ireland. The hill could be seen quite easily from the royal castle at Tara, and after the high king Laoghaire (Lear) noted the blaze in 433, he summoned the saint for an interview. St. Patrick explained his mission to Laoghaire, who gave him permission to preach the Christian faith but remained a heathen himself. Thus St. Patrick could begin his missionary work. Shortly after St. Patrick's death, St. Erc (died 514) founded a small cloister here, but it soon fell into obscurity. In the sixteenth century, Sir Christopher Flemming constructed a Franciscan abbey on the same spot, and the college associated with it served even

The barrow grave of Dowth.

under the English occupation as a training school for future priests.

Southeast of Slane, one finds the three prominent barrow graves in Ireland. The most notable is the passage grave of *Newgrange*. The site cannot be dated precisely, but it can be assumed to be roughly 4,500 years old. The hill of round stones covers an area of some 2 acres. Nearly 340 feet in diameter, the circular mound was originally surrounded by ninety-seven stone boulders. About 60 yards from the tomb, a wreath of thirty-five vertical menhirs once marked the site, but only twelve of the monoliths have survived. These stones formed a magical boundary designed to protect the illustrious person buried in the tomb from evil spirits. Most of the stones have been broken and have fallen over; only the four menhirs opposite the entrance still rise to their original height of 8 feet. The entrance, with its squared stone ornamented with a double spiral (illus. 6, page 35), lies in the southeastern part of the site. Forty-three upright stones roofed by stone slabs form a corri-

dor more than 60 feet long. It leads to the central tomb chamber (illus. 4 and 5, page 35), whose three side chambers produce a cruciform ground plan. Each of the chambers contains a stone hollowed out as a basin in which bones and jewelry were discovered. The absence of fire traces suggests that these ancient people did not cremate their corpses inside the tomb. The stones in the tomb chambers are decorated with various primitive ornaments such as double spirals —symbolic of the sun—zigzags, and serpentine lines. The stone that forms the roof of the right-hand side chamber reveals particularly beautiful designs. A number of ancient documents, including the Book of Ballymote, tell of an ancient burial place of the high kings, Brugh na Bóinne, and they probably refer to Newgrange. The early Irish considered the structure, already thousands of years old, to be the work and the residence of the chief Celtic god, Dagda.

Not far from Newgrange lies the barrow grave of *Dowth*. When one climbs down the ladders into its depths, one feels something of the mystery and danger of the past. Dowth has not been excavated completely, and it almost seems to repel visitors deliberately by being difficult to get about in. A stone passage leads underground to the burial chamber, which was used as a cultic site until well into Christian times. In the ninth century, the tombs in the Boyne Valley were plundered by Danes. As in Newgrange, one also sees here the ubiquitous double spirals, the absence of mortar in the masonry, the long corridor, and the sacrificial stone, discovered in the central chamber. The Book of Ballymote gave this tomb the name Duma Tresca.

Only people in good physical condition should attempt the somewhat tedious tour of the interior of the Dowth tomb. Others are advised to explore the more easily negotiated Newgrange.

The nearby *Knowth* tomb concealed its treasures for 4,000 years until its burial chamber was discovered on July 11, 1967. During the course of painstaking excavation, various ornamented stones, iron knives, and bones were discovered. As at Newgrange, a spiral-decorated squared stone stands in front of the entrance (illus. 11, page 37).

The two burial rooms of the tomb are unusual: the first, ringed with side niches, is circular and has a domed ceiling; the second, without niches, is V-shaped and covered with a flat roof. Knowth was a royal seat in the ninth and tenth centuries, and somewhat later, the Normans used it as a provisional fort.

Excavation of the area continues. In the past few years, archeologists have found fifteen subordinate tombs. Unfortunately, tourists will not be admitted inside in the near future.

Duleek, to the south of these tombs, deserves a visit because of its role in the history and development of the Irish church. In the fifth century, St. Patrick here installed St. Cianan as the head of his first relilgious foundation. When the high king Brian Ború died in the Battle of Clontarf, his body and those of his fallen attendants were first interred in the church at Duleek; later the king's remains were transferred with great pomp to Armagh for permanent burial. In the twelfth century, Duleek was a bishopric and enjoyed a new flowering, attested to by the ruins of St. Cianan's Church and the

The passage grave of Newgrange.

Augustinian abbey. The roadside cross that Jennet Dowdall commissioned in 1601 is interesting because it has virtually nothing in common with the Irish high crosses; rather it incorporates a Continental spirit. Its truncated arms extend only a short way beyond the shaft, which is ornamented with Gothic portraits of saints. On its east side, St. Peter, St. Patrick, and St. Ciaran are depicted; on the south, St. George, St. Andrew, St. Katherine, and St. Stephen; St. George with the dragon, Magdalene, St. John, and St. Thomas are also shown. Some of these figures had appeared on earlier high crosses, but others, such as Mary Magdalene and St. George, were first brought to Ireland by the medieval monks. It is odd that St. Patrick, rarely represented on the high crosses, is present here.

Jennet Dowdall is also responsible for the White Cross in *Athcarne*, which she had erected in memory of her third husband, William Bathe. From Athcarne, it is not far to Tara, one of the great royal seats of Europe, whose eventful history actually merits a book in itself.

Tara's origins reach back to the Bronze Age, but nothing survives from that period but a number of ring-shaped, grass-covered trenches and walls. The layout of the settlement poses a number of riddles, but historic documents permit us to piece together a magnificent picture. Through the centuries, more than 140 kings sought to control the fate of Ireland from this place, so it came to be called Teamhair na Ríogh, or Tara of the Kings. It was from Tara that glorious processions set out toward the Boyne Valley tombs, and here stands one of the two Irish coronation stones; the second, the Rock of Doon, is in Donegal.

The hill is only 501 feet high, but it nevertheless dominates the surroundings and offers a splendid view across the gardenlike landscape. From it, one can see the tower of the monastery at Slane. This panorama, of course, had great strategic value.

Every three years, the king organized a great six-day celebration to which everyone was invited. Colorful hordes of peasants and nobles arrived on the five main roads leading to Tara. Warriors (*flatha*), the *aes dána*, and the common folk (*bo airig*) were all represented. A historian (*ard ollamh*) carefully followed all the events in order to be able to record them accurately later. Magicians, charlatans, and pickpockets were just as numerous as the wise seers, Druids, and bards. There was a general truce during this festival, and anyone who broke it was subject to heavy punishment. People were expected to amuse themselves, drink, and eat to their heart's content. In the evening, they congregated in the large banqueting hall for further amusements. One cannot know precisely what this hall looked like, since no records or sketches are preserved from the Celtic period. However, one can form an approximate idea of it because the seating arrangement at table has been preserved in the books of Leinster and of Lecan. This plan not only suggests something about the size of the hall, but vividly reveals the social hierarchy of the time.

The banquet hall, some 650 feet long and 100 feet wide, may have resembled a Greek temple. Reports of large wooden halls, columns, and entrances decorated with gems suggest something of the crown's wealth. At one end of the table sat the clowns and jesters, artists and jugglers, and, across from them, the powerful clan of magicians. Following these, in forty-two separate divisions, came the goldsmiths, historians, judges, teachers, and—right next to the royal couple—the doctors. Although

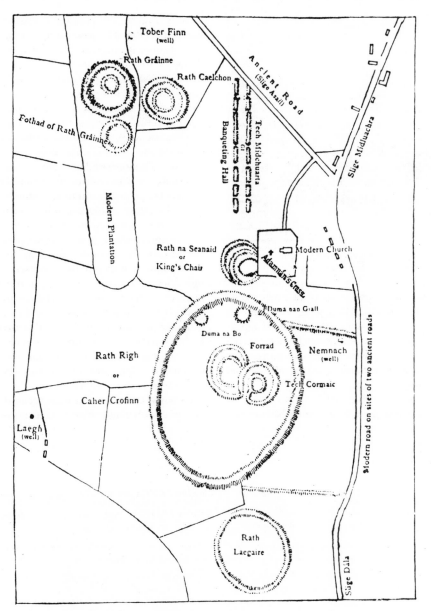

An early 20th-century plan of Tara.

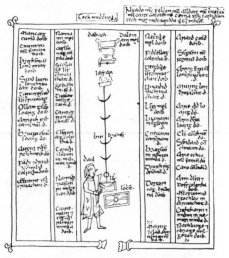

Seating arrangement of the banquet hall at Tara, from the Book of Leinster.

magicians were actually of higher rank than the doctors, they were "banished" to the far end of the table; it would appear that they were somewhat feared. On the opposite side were drummers, flutists, and other musicians, along with gladiators and charioteers.

Once the bards had sung the praises of their sovereigns and the Druids had intoned various magical formulas, the harpists began to perform. The Irish were especially skilled at this instrument. Their songs were divided into categories—lullabies and lays of mourning and of joy—that can still be applied to Irish folk music today. According to an old saying, everything at Tara revolved around music, and the lucky visitor can experience similar festivals in the more remote parts of the country even now, although on a more modest scale.

Among the many legends attached to Tara is one of the most beautiful love stories in world literature: *Dairmaid and Gráinne.* Its plot is somewhat comparable to that of Tristan and Isolde. Cormac MacArt, probably the most famous of the high kings, lived in the third century A.D. He possessed not only a legendary army, the Fenians, but all kinds of earthly riches as well. His greatest pride, though, was his beautiful and clever daughter Gráinne, whom he hoped to marry to the fabled hero and leader of the Fenians, Finn MacCool, as a reward for his deeds. Gráinne was little disposed to the aging, rough warrior. She had her eye on a younger soldier, Dairmaid, and was certain that he cared for her, too. With a magic potion,

Gráinne put the participants at a feast into a deep sleep so that she could escape with Dairmaid. Finn hunted for the pair for several years across the length and breadth of the island, but he finally consented to give up the contest. After many happy years together, Dairmaid and Gráinne invited Finn and the high king to a reconciliation feast, and in spite of Gráinne's warnings, Dairmaid took part in the hunt that was a part of the celebration. Everyone gathered at the foot of the great Ben Bulben, a large, flat-topped mountain, in order to bring down a wild boar. Dairmaid killed the boar, but he was seriously wounded and urgently needed help. Finn MacCool could have helped him, but he refused.

Cormac gathered the greatest men of his time at his court, founded schools of literature and goldsmithing shops, and oversaw the excellent military training of his soldiers. At the advanced age of ninety, he handed over the kingship to his son and died shortly afterward.

Another legendary event occurred in the fifth century. The high king felt that the power of the poets had become too great, and he called a *druim ceatt*, an assembly at Tara that lasted several days. St. Columba left the Scottish island of Iona in order to defend his fellow poets. The saint ultimately managed to restore peace between the thousand poets and the high king, but the poets were forced to give up most of their privileges. The people continued to value the poets, even in Christian times, for the cynical taunts they used to criticize injustices. According to legend, the poets possessed the power to wound or even to kill their enemies by means of speech.

Today, one can best survey Tara from the air, where its complicated layout can be disentangled. At the center of an oval space, surrounded by the Ráth na Ríogh (Wall of the Kings), is Teach Cormaic (Cormac's House), in the center of which, in turn, a rounded stone thrusts upward. This is Lia Fáil, the coronation stone, which was ceremoniously consulted for its judgments. If the stone, thousands of years old, failed to respond, any given investiture was considered invalid. This practice went back to the

Tara.

161

Milesian Queen Tea, the legendary founder of Tara. Tea's grave may have formed the original foundation of the residence. The Lia Fáil now in Tara is doubtless a copy; presumably the original, after being carried to Scone in Scotland, was set into the English throne at Westminster.

The broad circle next to Cormac's House comprised the Forradh, the assembly place; to the south, somewhat outside the wall, lie the remains of King Laoghaire's House. To the north, within the wall, lies the Mound of the Hostages (Dumha na nGiall), a 4,000-year-old passage grave with similar ornamentation to that at Newgrange and to other tombs. Historians ascribe its name to the many hostages whom Cormac captured from all parts of the island and put to death. In a fort outside the Ráth na Ríogh, the saints Patrick, Ruedhan, and Adamnán convened their synods.

Just next to the Fort of the Synods, in the middle of a small cemetery that contains the stump of the cross of St. Adamnán, one finds the "newest" building at Tara, scarcely more than a few centuries old, the simple St. Patrick's Church.

A bit farther to the north, one can make out the outlines of the banqueting hall, discussed above. Even though this structure may not have been as imposing as Greek temples or Roman palaces, its significance is nonetheless unquestioned; Ireland did not produce any other monumental building.

The rubble-covered graves (*Claoin Fhearta*) to the west of the hall were the scene of a massacre when the king of Leinster revolted against the authority of Tara in 222 A.D. The main force of the Fenians was on the way to secure peace elsewhere, and thus 3,000 people, among them 30 princesses, were killed.

The last high king of Ireland, Roderick O'Connor, had his troops camp at Tara in 1170 before his decisive battle against the Anglo-Normans. His motive was probably to impress upon them the earnestness of their endeavor and to give them courage.

Even after defeat, the memory of Tara continued to live in the hearts of the Irish. During the great famine in the nineteenth century, more than 1 million Irish made a pilgrimage to a worship service held at Tara, and today, the stream of pilgrims and tourists to the spot sometimes seems unabated. Visitors may leave Tara somewhat disappointed because there are no spectacular buildings or works of art here; only a knowledge of history can enable one to appreciate the full significance of the site.

Driving west from Tara, one soon approaches *Trim* and spots the outlines of powerful Trim Castle (Ath Truim), one of the few Anglo-Norman ruins from the close of the twelfth century that were not altered by later restoration (illus. 73, page 178).

As early as the fifth century, a church consecrated to the Virgin Mary stood at Trim. It was founded by St. Patrick, who installed St. Loman as its bishop. The many-storied Yellow Steeple on the bank opposite the castle marks the original site of this church. Additional church structures are to be found in the immediate neighborhood. A stroll along High Street and then to the left into narrow Church Lane leads one to St. Patrick's Church. This church was restored in the nineteenth century. It stands, along with its 500-year-old round tower, in the midst of grave slabs and stones.

Black Friary, a cloister outside the former town wall, was endowed by Geoffrey de Joinville and administered by the Dominicans, who also participated substantially in the politics of the country. A number of parliaments passed measures humiliating to the Irish. For example, in 1446, it was de-

Trim Castle.

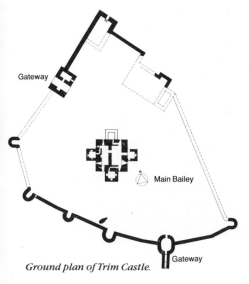

Ground plan of Trim Castle.

creed that all Irishmen had to wear their beards in the English fashion and were forbidden to wear yellow shirts. The eventful history of Trim Castle shows that the English had to fight hard against the rebellion.

Henry II, the English monarch and conqueror, sent one of his faithful vassals, Hugh de Lacy, to Trim, presented him with a great deal of land, and had him build a major fortress beside the River Boyne. The structure was built quickly and completed in 1173. The strong towers and walls of Trim Castle formed a visible sign of the power that was a thorn in the side of every Irishman, whose Tara lay in ruins. When Hugh de Lacy returned to England, he left the fortress in the trusted hands of Hugh Tyrell. King Roderick O'Connor capitalized on de Lacy's absence and assembled an army at Tara. His force besieged Trim Castle and destroyed it. The earl of Pembroke, the legendary Strongbow, was summoned to aid the defenders; although he rushed to the scene, he found nothing but ruins when he arrived. He avenged his countrymen by putting a hundred of O'Connor's soldiers to death. Hugh Tyrell, who had fled, managed to rebuild Trim Castle before Hugh de Lacy's return, but de Lacy did not have long to enjoy his possession. An enraged worker beheaded him with an axe in Durrow because he wanted to dismantle the monastery of Durrow and use its stones to construct another castle. Stones from the walls around the churches of Newtown Trim, a mile down the river, had already met this fate.

The main square structure of the fortress was provided with a projecting tower on each side, and the ground plan is thus twenty-sided. These towers were not built at the corners, as was customary, but were located in the very center of each side. The north tower has unfortunately collapsed, and the remaining portions are also extremely precarious, so one is strongly urged not to climb in it. One must be satisfied with a glance into the living space with its fireplace on the ground floor and the former chapel in the east tower before turning to the remarkably well-preserved walls of the large courtyard. From these, one can enjoy a broad panorama. To the right, across the river, stands the Sheep Gate, a fragment of the town wall built by Roger Mortimer in 1359.

Downstream, the badly deteriorated cathedrals of St. Peter and St. Paul·in *Newtown*

Cathedral of St. Peter and St. Paul, Newtown Trim.

Trim come into view. In an annex, of which only the gable and 20-inch-high walls remain, is the beautiful double tomb of Sir Lucas Dillon and his wife. This sixteenth-century sarcophagus remains distinctive in spite of the considerable weathering of its soft stone. The Augustinian monastery of Newtown Trim formerly comprised a church with side aisles, two transepts, and a choir, to which the square cloister garden, a refectory, and housekeeping buildings were attached. The ivy-covered ruins near the small bridge are the remains of a hospital.

On the way to Kells, one passes *Bective Abbey*, a two-story cloister ruin with large corner towers that were built as fortifications during the troubled twelfth century. Scarcely any other abbey in Ireland is as well preserved; only the roofs and some of the partition walls are missing. The Cistercian monks came here from Mellifont and were subject to the control of the mother cloister at Clairvaux, in the south of France. A free-standing row of arcades, the only one in Ireland, separates the church and the cemetery. The slain Hugh de Lacy is said to be buried near these arches. The lord's head, to be sure, was buried in St. Thomas's in Dublin, resulting in a conflict between the two cloisters that had to be resolved by the pope. The break between the pope and Henry VIII doomed Bective Abbey, and its monks were either killed or driven away.

After passing through the hospitable village of Navan, one takes the main road northwest toward *Kells* and its venerable monastery. The history of Kells is an eventful and stormy one. The remains of its churches and crosses attest to the culture of the early monks. St.

Bective Abbey.

165

Ruins at Kells.

Columba founded a monastery here shortly before he went to the island of Iona to establish another one in 563. The schools at both Kells and Iona enjoyed an excellent reputation, even during the saint's lifetime. St. Columba's special concern in Iona was the school of scribes that produced the most beautiful works of Irish book illumination.

Shortly after 800, the abbot Cellach had the derelict cloister rebuilt, and various reliquaries of St. Columba could be transferred to it by 877. By all accounts the greatest treasure of the monastery was the Book of Kells, now in Trinity College Library, Dublin (illus. 26 and 27, pages 42 and 43).

The monks protected their treasure during countless attacks, yet in spite of all precautions, the book was stolen from the sacristy in 1007. The brothers' sorrow must have been great, but even greater was their joy when the book was discovered unharmed in a field two and a half months later. The thief apparently placed no value on the book itself since only its precious gold covers were missing. The monastery also survived two fires, in 1111 and 1156. These blazes spared the cloister's treasures and allowed the spiritual life of the establishment to continue uninterrupted. The importance of Kells increased when the synod of 1152 redefined the ecclesiastical provinces and made Kells the seat of a diocese —although only briefly.

Seeing the round tower and the crosses at the top of the hill ranks among the greatest experiences of any tour of Ireland. Unfortunately, the tower is now missing its conical roof, and the ornamentation of its doorway is considerably weathered. The elegant structure dates from the period before 1076; this is known because historical records from this period report the murder of one of the high king's heirs in this tower. Near the tower stands the South Cross, from the ninth century; its strangely blurred ornaments flow into each other in a most uncommon manner (illus. 47, page 117).

Base: A procession, various animals, and ornaments.

South side: Adam and Eve, Cain and Abel, the three young men in the fiery furnace, Daniel in the lion's den; left crossarm: the sacrifice of Isaac; right crossarm: Peter and Paul in the desert; top: David with his harp and the miracle of the loaves.

West side: Crucifixion and Last Judgment; crossarm: David killing lions and bears.

About 100 feet to the northwest is the stump of a high cross with particularly beautiful ornaments. Its east side depicts the baptism of Christ in the Jordan (a rare theme), the Marriage at Cana, David with his harp, Christ teaching in the Temple, and, in its center, Jesus entering Jerusalem. The west side shows Adam and Eve, a delightful Noah's ark, and several unidentifiable scenes. (Positive identification of the scenes on high crosses is difficult and is often a matter of dispute among art historians. Generally, a given sequence can be explained in terms of either the Bible or events from the artist's own time. Just as the monks patterned their lives after the desert saints mentioned in the Bible, so did they take their artistic motifs primarily from Old Testament stories.)

An unfinished cross next to the new church permits one to study something of the sculptors' techniques before proceeding to St. Columba's House behind the church square (illus. 69, page 128). This building, made of squared stones and with a pointed roof, is reminiscent of St. Kevin's Kitchen in Glendalough (Wicklow). A ladder out of the gloomy main room leads to the three-part attic in which St. Columba is believed to have said his prayers and worked on illuminated manuscripts. The building is surely of more recent date, however; it probably belongs to the second period of building at this monastery in the ninth century. St. Columba's House once stood within the precinct of the cloister, which extended far beyond the present-day cemetery and accommodated several thousand monks.

The Market Cross (illus. 48, page 118) in the village was created much later than the two examples described above, and it seems somewhat out of place among the small houses. An inscription relates that Robert Balfe had the cross erected in 1688. The themes and the execution of the Market Cross have little in common with the Irish high crosses of the seventh to twelfth centuries; they show rather a clear Continental influence.

Base: Battle scenes, riders, and animals.

East side: Christ in the tomb guarded by soldiers, Goliath, Adam and Eve, Cain and Abel, Daniel menaced by lions (center), and the sacrifice of Isaac (left).

West side: Adoration of the saints, marriage at Cana, miracle of the loaves, and, as almost always, a relief of the Crucifixion.

South side: The healing of the blind man,

Animals and fabulous beasts from the base of the Market Cross, Kells.

167

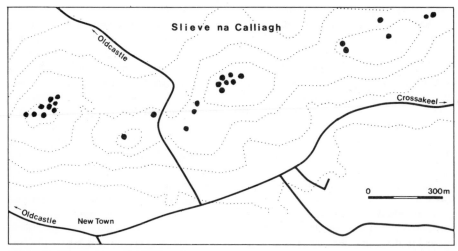

Site plan of the passage graves of Loughcrew.

and Moses receiving the Ten Commandments.

Irish foundations all over Europe attest to the immense influence that monasteries like Kells had, for it was from here and similar settlements that monks set out for the Continent.

Along the road toward Oldcastle, one passes the Slieve na Calliagh (Mountain of the Witches), at *Loughcrew* (illus. 3, page 34). Its more than thirty passage graves, of the same type as those in the Boyne Valley, comprise the last stop in the culturally rich landscape of Meath. The graves are located on two hills, one on either side of the park-

ing area. A walk to the graves is rewarding, for portions of their roofs are missing, allowing one to see their exposed passageways and chambers. The country surrounding these graves, which rise like beehives, serves as pasturage for horses and sheep. Spirals, which were used as symbols as early as the Stone Age, ornament the entrances to the graves, which the Irish held to be the openings into underground dwellings of the banished Tuatha dé Danaan.

West of Longcrew lie the remains of *Granard*, probably the largest motte and bailey fort in Ireland, which was surrounded by a large ditch.

Westmeath

Athlone—Lough Ree— Inchbofin

The counties of Westmeath and Offaly are also part of Leinster, but because of their

location in the center of Ireland, it is advisable to drive north out of Meath into Donegal, postponing one's visit to Athlone and Clonmacnoise—by no means to be missed—until one returns from the north and can simply turn toward the interior at Galway. For the sake of completeness, however, these two counties will be discussed here.

Athlone lies in the center of Ireland, commanding the southern tip of *Lough Ree* (roughly 15 miles long) and boasting an impressive Norman castle beside the Shannon. Those who have rented a boat already or who choose to do so here can ride out to the island of *Inchbofin*, where there are ruins of an early religious settlement. Its two churches have long since lost their roofs, as have most structures from this period, and now stand exposed to the constant winds. The doorway and windows of the small south church are well worth seeing. Across from the other church, there is a baptismal font built into a wall fragment. Returning to the mainland, one now follows the winding River Shannon downstream

through its picturesque plain and comes to Clonmacnoise, central Ireland's monastic settlement.

Athlone Castle.

Offaly

Clonmacnoise—Stone of Clonfinlough—Durrow

Clonmacnoise (illus. 51–54, pages 118–120) constitutes an imposing open-air museum. Its nine churches, two round towers, and three high crosses, along with numerous grave crosses, provide a splendid overview of Irish art. The area is often overrun by tourists who make their first stop here after leaving Shannon Airport. When hiking around here, one should also be warned to watch the sky even in fair weather, for brief but violent rain showers are frequent.

The monastery was founded by St. Ciaran in 548. The surviving monuments were created by monastic artists around the end of

the tenth century, when the cloister school housed some 6,000 students and offered university instruction as well.

Two books relate the repeated plundering of Clonmacnoise. The Book of Tigernach, from the eleventh century, and the Book of the Dun Cow, from the twelfth, record almost thirty attacks by Gaels, thirteen plunderings by the Vikings, and six by Anglo-Normans. The Viking prince Turgesius came up the Shannon with dragon boats in 845. Once the precinct had been conquered, he ordered his wife, Ota, to make a sacrifice on its consecrated altar and declaim heathen oracles. Its final collapse began in the sixteenth century, when the English caused nearly all Catholic cloisters to be dissolved.

There are many gravestones here; some

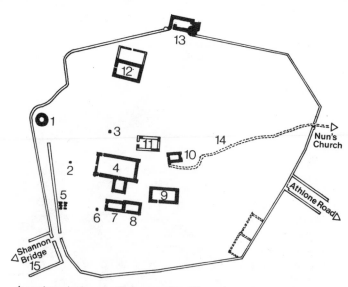

Plan of Clonmacnoise.
1. *Round Tower*
2. *Inscription Cross*
3. *North Cross*
4. *Cathedral*
5. *Grave slabs*
6. *South Cross*
7. *Temple Doolin*
8. *Temple Hurpan*
9. *Temple Ri*
10. *Temple Kieran*
11. *Temple Kelly*
12. *Temple Connor*
13. *Temple Finghir*
14. *Footpath*
15. *Parking lot*

bear inscriptions in Ogham script. There is also a round tower built a thousand years ago and restored after a fire two centuries later. The most famous cross at the abbey dates from the same period. It is known as the Inscription Cross, or Flann's Cross (illus. 54, page 120), and is a Bible cross whose workmanship and choice of themes resemble those of the Muiredach Cross at Monasterboice.

West side: Soldiers guarding the tomb, an arrest, the betrayal and Crucifixion of Christ.

East side: Dairmuid (Diarmait) MacCerbaill, the church's benefactor, assists St. Ciaran in erecting the first corner pillar of the church. Christ in glory sits enthroned among righteous souls playing instruments and evil ones condemned to hell.

South side: David playing his harp, and a bishop symbolizing dignity and power.

North side: Another bishop, a piper, and a falconer.

Base: Horsemen, hunting scenes, depictions of animals, and the inscription "[C]olman dorro[ini in chroi]ssa ar [in rig Flai]nd" ["Colman erected this cross for King Flann"].

Next to Temple Doolin stands the South Cross. This is essentially an ornamental cross, although it does have some figures on it, including a Crucifixion on the west side. A third cross, only partially preserved, stands to the north. It provides a link between the two styles, for its reliefs contain far more than mere ornamentation.

Various churches stand at the heart of Clonmacnoise. Foremost among them is the cathedral with its inscription cross. This church, built by the abbot Colman Conailleach and the high king Flann, boasts a beautiful Romanesque doorway and contains the tomb of Roderick O'Connor, the last of the high kings, whose struggle against the English was recounted in connection with Trim (see p. 164). His tomb lay in the original sacristy; the present one is scarcely more than 300 years old. The existing doorway was added during rebuilding in 1330, and it features statues of St. Patrick, St. Dominic, and St. Francis.

From Temple Kieran, behind the cathedral, a path leads beyond the cloister precinct to the Nun's Church. A Romanesque doorway and a number of especially fine ornaments distinguish this church from 1166. It is well worth continuing on to the ruined Norman castle on the bank of the Shannon. Photographers especially will not want to miss it.

Only 2 miles from Clonmacnoise lies the huge *Stone of Clonfinlough*. Badly weathered prehistoric symbols, crosses, and stylized human figures embellish the massive block of limestone. Similar stones have been found in the northern part of the Iberian Peninsula. (To reach the stone from Clonmacnoise, take the road to Athlone. After 2 miles, take the first turnoff to the south, following it until you come to a church. A marked path leads from the church to the stone.)

At the northern border of Offaly, on the road from Tullamore to Kilbeggan, lies *Durrow*, the former monastery where the famous manuscript of the same name was

The sacrifice of Isaac from the Bible Cross, Durrow.

created; this book is now one of the greatest treasures of Trinity College Library, Dublin. St. Columba founded the abbey of Durrow in 553, it later came into the possession of the Augustinians, and it was destroyed during the Middle Ages. The main attraction at Durrow today is its tenth-century Bible cross reliefs. Near the cross are several gravestones with the repeated inscription "Or do"... ("a prayer for... ") and a cross fragment.

ULSTER

Six counties in the historic province of Ulster—Armagh, Down, Fermanagh, Tyrone, Antrim, and Londonderry—today comprise the British part of Ireland. Because of the uneasy political situation there, it will be described only partially. Driving through the border countryside is quite safe. In fact, Northern Ireland is peaceful except for the cities, especially Belfast, Newry, and Londonderry. Those driving northward from Kells would be well advised to take a side trip to the ancient northern royal fortress, Eamhain Macha, located on the maps as Navan Fort. The fort lies only a few miles across the border along the road between Monaghan and Armagh. (Counties Cavan, Donegal, and Monaghan, also in Ulster, are part of the Republic of Ireland today.)

Fermanagh (Northern Ireland)

White Island—Devenish—Boa Island

On *White Island*, in Lower Lough Erne, there is an abbey in whose walls eight small statues are mounted (illus. 13 and 14, page 38). They were only discovered in this century, and they are difficult to date or identify. It may be that they depict the seven deadly sins, but this interpretation does not

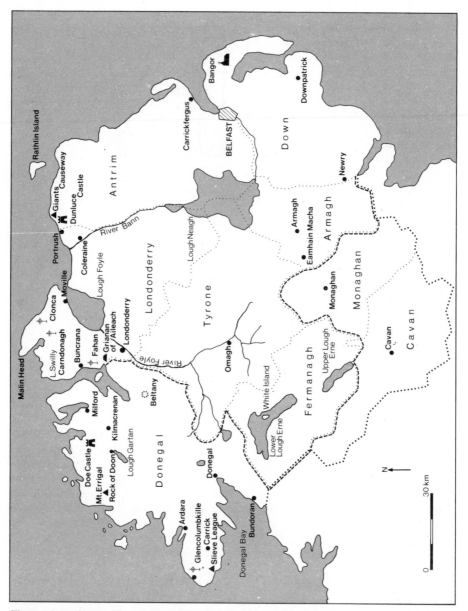

The province of Ulster. The counties of Donegal, Cavan, and Monaghan belong to the Republic of Ireland; the six counties of Armagh, Down, Antrim, Tyrone, Fermanagh, and Londonderry comprise Northern Ireland, which is part of Great Britain.

explain the eighth, and seemingly Mongoloid, figure.

White Island is difficult to reach. One can be rowed across in the evening from Milltown, or one can rent a motorboat at the yacht club at Kesh. One should have the route clearly explained on a map, and one should not forget an umbrella and rainwear.

In the southern part of the lake, not far from Enniskillen, is *Devenish*—an island accessible only by boat. It contains a well-preserved 80-foot-high round tower that belonged to the monastic foundation of St. Molaise, from the sixth century (illus. 109, page 229).

Boa Island, in the northern part of Lower Lough Erne, is easier to reach. A bridge leads across the narrow waterway that separates the island from the lake shore. On Boa Island, well away from the road and near the remains of an ancient cemetery, two early Celtic figures stand hidden among the swamp vegetation (illus. 28, page 44). (*Note*: Drive slowly along the straight section of road, for it is easy to miss the sign pointing off to the south. Rugged shoes are necessary here.) The remarkably austere and crude figures, as high as gravestones, reveal the same stylistic elements as examples in Germany and in Provence. In order to get from Boa Island to County Donegal, one has to return to Kesh and cross the border on the mainland.

Donegal

St. Patrick's Island—Donegal —Beltany—Grianán of Aileach —Londonderry (Northern Ireland) —Dunluce Castle (Northern Ireland)—Giant's Causeway (Northern Ireland)— Clonca—Malin Head— Carndonagh—Fahan—Rock of Doon—Ardara—Glencolumbkille—Cliffs of Bunglass

North of Pettigo, on *St. Patrick's Island* (Station Island) in Lough Derg, one of the most rigorous pilgrimages takes place annually. The saint used to fast here, and tens of thousands of pilgrims assemble at this spot on St. Patrick's Day, and they do without food, sleep, and even shoes for a three-day period of penance and prayer. During this exercise, only pilgrims may set foot on the island. Observers are forbidden, and fishermen will not transport tourists to the island then for any price.

After a short drive, one reaches the town of *Donegal*. The castle that gave the county its name towers above the houses and the River Eask in the center of the town. Its massive tower was built by O'Donnell around 1500, and it is partially decorated with ornamental bands. The three-story Manor House dates from around 1620. To the south of Donegal, the Franciscans constructed an abbey that the English later fortified and expanded. In the seventeenth century, the abbey burned to the ground when a powder magazine exploded, but it was rebuilt shortly afterward.

The atmosphere in Donegal is quite different from that of the towns to the south. The raw climate and the poor soil do not permit cultivation, and industrialization is not very advanced. The land is poor and thinly settled; there are scarcely any ways to earn a living except for working in the peat bogs. Only a few people seem to thrive on this difficult and monotonous life. Most

Donegal Castle.

move to the cities—Dublin, Cork, even London—or emigrate to the United States. Since this area has produced very few works of art, the tourist is left to admire the changing colors of the mountains, which manifest every shade from a pale yellow to a blackish brown.

On the way to the Inishowen Peninsula, it is best to turn off at Raphoe to *Beltany* in order to see the Druid circle at the top of the hill. This ring of over sixty stones—a number of them now missing—was a cultic site high above the surrounding landscape.

An even better panorama is provided far-

ther north by the hill near Londonderry that boasts the ring fort *Grianán of Aileach* (*Grianán* means "sun house"). No signposts are required here; even at a distance one can see the wall rising above the summit of the brown mountain. The circular wall is about 16 feet high, and its diameter is roughly 130 feet. On the inside the wall is stepped, and one has to climb a number of narrow stairways to get to the top (illus. 64 and 65, page 124). The entrance is often closed with an iron gate; if so, one should try to scale the wall from the outside, for the panorama over the mouths of the rivers Swilly and Foyle must not be missed.

A 19th-century view of Londonderry.

Unlike the fjords in Norway, which were carved by glaciers, these 12- to 18-mile notches into the land were dug by the rivers themselves. The landscape around the "sun house," whose age is unknown, gleams with misty green, interrupted only by the brilliant blue of the watercourses and the gray smoke to the east, which permits one to sense, though not to see, the restless industrial city of Londonderry.

Anyone wishing to visit the two Northern Irish counties of Londonderry and Antrim must turn east here. The city of *Londonderry* is a typical British industrial city; it is only too familiar from newscasts as the scene of bitter fighting. St. Columba had established a monastery near Londonderry before moving on to Kells.

The heart of Londonderry is protected by a powerful fortress whose walls are interrupted by four gates. James I presented the city of Derry to the Corporation of London, encouraged Protestants to settle there, and commissioned the building of the walls that still stand today. One of the gates was replaced by a more elaborate entrance resembling a triumphal arch, decorated with reliefs, in about 1789 as a memorial to the great siege of Londonderry in 1688–1689.

It is now known as Bishop's Gate. Two hundred years ago, a number of fashionable residential streets were laid out for Protestants outside the city walls. The sole ornamentation of the houses in this section, generally one story high, was their decorated doorways.

When the famine broke out in the 1840s, many Irishmen from Londonderry tried to make their way to the United States. But there were available jobs in the new textile factories, so a number of Catholics stayed on. Thus there developed, next to the elegant Protestant quarter, a much poorer working-class district.

Not far from the cliff-lined coast, one drives as far as Coleraine along the River Bann, which forms the boundary between Londonderry and Antrim. At Portrush, one reaches the sea, then drives eastward until, just behind the large golf course, the bizarre outlines of *Dunluce Castle* come into view (illus. 113, page 231). In about 1300, an earl of Ulster, Richard de Burgh, built the castle on top of a much older coastal fort to which the floor below the courtyard, hewn out of the cliff, may well have belonged. During the next few centuries, Dunluce Castle was repeatedly enlarged by the addition of fireplaces, towers, and gateways. In about 1652, after the defeat of the Catholics by Cromwell's troops, its residents abandoned the castle, and Dunluce thus became another ruin on the cliffs above the Atlantic.

Only a few miles farther to the east, the *Giant's Causeway*, a massive natural jetty, falls off toward the sea. These remarkable cliffs were formed as the molten basalt from prehistoric volcanic eruptions crystallized into thousands of hexagonal columns. This formation, whose blocks of stone glow with the most diverse colors, is one of the most magnificent natural spectacles in Ireland.

Dunluce Castle.

72. Kilmacduagh Abbey, cathedral and round tower, 11th–12th century, Galway. ▷

73. Trim Castle, the powerful Norman fortress on the River Boyne, 12th century, Meath.

74. Ormond Castle, the former residence of the Butlers of Ormond, built in 1192, Tipperary.

75. Athassel Priory, Tipperary.

76, 77. Jerpoint Abbey, Kilkenny—a Cistercian foundation from the close of the 12th century. The figures on the columns are the work of Rory O'Tunney; sarcophagus with depictions of saints.

78. The Viking St. Laurence Gate, early 10th century, Drogheda, Louth.

79. Ruins of the Franciscan abbey, founded in 1351, Ross Errily, Galway.

80. Mellifont Abbey, Louth—remains of the church, monastery courtyard, and basin.

81. Octagonal basin, Mellifont Abbey.

82. Quin Abbey, Clare, a Franciscan abbey, 14th–15th century.

83, 84. St. Canice's Cathedral, Kilkenny.

85. View from Cashel of St. Dominick's Abbey, Tipperary.

86. Rock of Cashel, Tipperary. This powerful fortress of the kings and later the archbishops of Munster is visible from a great distance.

87. Cormac's Chapel, 1227–1234, Rock of Cashel, Tipperary.

88. The well-preserved round tower at Glendalough, Wicklow, is 108 feet tall. [

89. Churchyard and St. Kevin's Church with bell tower, Glendalough, Wicklow.

90. Protestant parish church and ruins of the priory of the Blessed Virgin and St. Columba, Inistioge, Kilkenny.

91. Landscape near Tintern Abbey, Wexford.

92. Ennis Friary, Clare, founded by Donchad
Cairbreach O'Brien in 1242.

93. Nave with tombs and lancet windows, Ennis Friary

94. Portal archivolts, richly ornamented with stylized plant and animal motifs, Clonfert, Galway.

95. Clonfert—portal of the cathedral, late 12th century.

96. Romanesque portal, 12th century, Killeshin, Laois.

97. Romanesque portal, Dysert O'Dea, Clare.

98. Romanesque portal, Cong Abbey, Mayo.

99. Human and animal heads, detail of the outside archivolts, Dysert O'Dea, Clare.

A 19th-century view of Giant's Causeway.

Back toward Donegal, the route takes one either back through Londonderry or, by the small ferry from Magilligan Point across the narrowest spot on Lough Foyle, to Greencastle, on the Inishowen Peninsula.

At Muff, the road reaches the shore of Lough Foyle, follows it until Moville, and then continues to the north. At Gleneely, in the valley of the same name, a road turns off toward the lesser-known high crosses of Carrowmore and the remains of *Clonca*, a monastic foundation of St. Buodan (illus. 12, page 38). Its ruined church is only a few hundred years old. The slender shaft of a high cross is preserved from an earlier period. The geometric ornaments are interrupted by a very few pictorial reliefs. Its east side depicts the miracle of the loaves; the west side, two men praying. The style of the work suggests that it was created in the tenth century.

Via Culdaff, with its Druid circle, one reaches Malin. In good weather—which the Irish take to include practically any conditions short of a hurricane—it is worth making the short side trip to *Malin Head*, the northern cape of Ireland, where there is a small parking area. From there, a westward hike of slightly more than half a mile leads to Hell's Hole, a narrow cut into the cliff. Here, at ebb tide, the water is a radiant green. One can easily imagine that at flood tide or during a storm the chasm can indeed become infernal chaos.

One has now reached the most distant point of the journey and must turn southward.

St. Patrick's Cross, the oldest high cross in Ireland (illus. 30, page 45), stands at the entrance to the village of *Carndonagh*, right

193

beside the road to Buncrana. In the seventh century, the first Irish Christians developed this early form out of the previous Celtic standing stones. The cross arms are already present, suggested by graceful indentations, although the ring has not yet developed. Intertwining ribbon ornaments, the favored Celtic forms, as well as primitive depictions of human figures decorate both the cross itself and a number of smaller stones.

The road to Buncrana runs upward until the Gap of Mamore, then descends into the valley on the other side. Anyone who takes the opportunity to hike in this charming, open landscape for a day or longer will be rewarded with endless impressions and memorable views.

After Buncrana with its fourteenth-century Norman castle, known as O'Doherty's Keep, one comes to *Fahan*, where there is a stone resembling a high cross but whose arms are short stumps that barely project from the body (illus. 29, page 45). Like the cross at Carndonagh, this is in fact a preparatory form. Near the foot of the Fahan Stone are some figural ornaments that are probably the earliest to have been carved on a high cross, circa seventh century. Ornamental crosses attained their full flowering about a century later, but one does not come upon figures again until the Bible crosses of the ninth to eleventh centuries.

South of Fahan, one leaves the Inishowen Peninsula and soon arrives in Letterkenny, where there are pleasant places to stay. From here, one can either follow the coast via Milford or take the mountainous route into the interior of Donegal, passing Conwal Church and visiting the home of the celebrated St. Columba. On the nearby Lough Gartan, St. Columba built his first monastery, of which nothing remains today. From this elongated mountain lake, one proceeds to the *Rock*

of Doon, the coronation stone of the O'Donnell clan at the foot of the Kilmacrenan. On windy nights, pretenders to the throne had to subject themselves to the judgment of the stone. Only when the stone confirmed the right of the would-be king with a loud roar were they permitted to accede to the office. The laws of the clan were read aloud to the new king, and his taboos were determined. No king was free of taboos. Some were permitted to ride only in a given direction around their castle on certain days, others could participate in hunting only at specified times, and so on—a shrewd and effective protection against misuses of power by the monarch. Naturally, it must have been the wind that caused the stone to roar, a sound that was drowned out after the ceremony by the repeated shouts of the name O'Donnell by a hundred throats.

Doe Castle, a small structure from the fifteenth century, lies right on the bay at Sheep Haven just before Creeslough. Since Catholic Ireland had been opposed to England in its struggles with Spain, this castle was allocated to the survivors of the Spanish Armada whose boats were destroyed in Irish waters.

The sunsets that give the countryside a deep red glow caused this portion of Donegal to be known as "Bloody Fireland." Following the coast, one comes to *Ardara*. Here, tweeds and other woolens of the highest quality are manufactured, and the prices are far lower than in Dublin. With luck, one can buy tasteful souvenirs and handicrafts for very little indeed. The road then leads through the valley of Glengesh up to Glengesh Pass. Beware of overheating; many a car has broken down during this climb!

One next comes to the valley of *Glencolumbkille*, the goal of countless pilgrims each year on St. Columba's feast day, June

9. Nothing is left of the monastery of St. Columba, but standing stones strewn over a distance of more than 3 miles serve as markers for the pilgrimage. One of the loveliest ornamented stones stands near the church. Small megalithic burial mounds are scattered about the valley. Along the road to Malin More lies Cloghanmore, a large open passage grave. Near Farranmacbride is another, Mannernamortee.

The broad, sandy beach of the bay is interrupted by cliffs and is reminiscent of a number of spots along the coast of Spain. But the temperature serves to remind one of the latitude, and those who prefer the temperatures of the south will hardly think of going into the water for a swim.

However, for those who enjoy a whiskey by the fire late in the evening, there is no reason to despair. In the small villages throughout Ireland closing hours are rare —or at least they are not strictly adhered to. Generally, the owner of a pub lives right behind it, so purchases are possible until quite late at night.

Irish whiskey (with an "e") is not the same as its Scottish counterpart. The taste is finer and much milder, almost resembling a mellow cognac. Together with the equally renowned Guinness Stout, the various brands of whiskey make up the national drinks that should be sampled. For women, drinking in public is often difficult. Women are permitted in many pubs when accompanied by a man, but there is no general rule.

Glencolumbkille is a pleasant place to stay, and its visitors are mostly from England. Countless vacation bungalows, complete with kitchens, are available here at very modest prices. The large bungalow settlement is more expensive than the private cottages, which generally accommodate six people; but the latter are usually booked up long in advance.

Leaving Glencolumbkille, the road continues on to the *Cliffs of Bunglass*. At Carrick, one turns off toward Teelin, on the bay of the same name, where a narrow mountainous road leads to a kind of parking place. From here, it is an impressive sight when the ebb tide breaks against the vertical cliffs over 300 feet high. One Man's Pass, a well-worn path, winds from here up to Slieve League, the summit of which cannot be seen from the cliffs. Only sturdy hikers should attempt the difficult route, for the climb takes several hours and requires stamina. One must take food and drink.

Returning to the town of Donegal, one ends the tour of this northernmost county; and just beyond the seaside resort of Bundoran, with its golf course and some twenty hotels in every price range, one enters the next province, Connacht.

CONNACHT

This former kingdom, covered with lakes, is much more developed as a tourist center than the north. It especially attracts anglers and golfers from all over the world, and its climate and vegetation hint of warmer, more southerly regions. The golf course at Rosses Point in Sligo is one of the best in the British Isles, and a number of riding clubs rent horses for quite reasonable fees.

Leitrim

Connacht's northernmost county possesses a coastline only a few miles long, but it offers excellent country for sportsmen and hikers who want to avoid the main roads.

Via Hamilton Manor, it is possible to take a side trip to the Franciscan monastery of Creevelea, near Dromahair, visit the charming Lough Allen, and view the megalithic tomb of Carracloona, near Kilticlogher, on the way back. The coast road, however, leads directly to Sligo.

Sligo

Creevykeel—Inishmurray—Drumcliff—Sligo—Ballymote Castle

Two mountains tower above this flat and densely settled green landscape, so faithfully evoked by William Butler Yeats in his poems. The Ox Mountains lie between the county town, Sligo, and Ballina; but first, just across the border, stands the commanding table mountain of Ben Bulben with its famous green slopes and brown rock outcroppings. It was here that the story of Dairmaid and Gráinne ended with Dairmaid's struggle with the boar of Ben Bulben and the deaths of both.

Ancient legends from the third saga cycle relate a number of battles, but here it is appropriate to tell only one, the *Táin Bó Cuailnge*, or Cattle Raid of Cooley. The legendary Queen Medb, whose huge cairn grave crowns nearby Knocknaera, had a favorite white bull that ran off to join the herds of her husband, Ailill. She therefore tried to replace it with a bull of the same quality. When she stole the black-horned bull of Cooley, the pride of Ulster, a feud ensued in which the hero of the second saga cycle, Cúchulainn, played a decisive role. Armed with just a sling, like David, Cúchulainn managed to hold back the queen's army by himself for several hours. Only after the two bulls themselves had entered into the fracas and the bull of Cooley had valiantly died was peace restored.

A passage grave at *Creevykeel* is remarkable for the dimensions of its large chamber. It dates from a much earlier period than this saga—the third millennium B.C.; this grave has only one side chamber.

One of the main attractions of Sligo is the small island of *Inishmurray*, off the coast, with its well-preserved monastery (illus. 31,

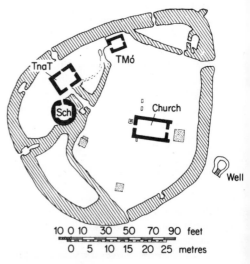

Plan of Inishmurray monastery.

196

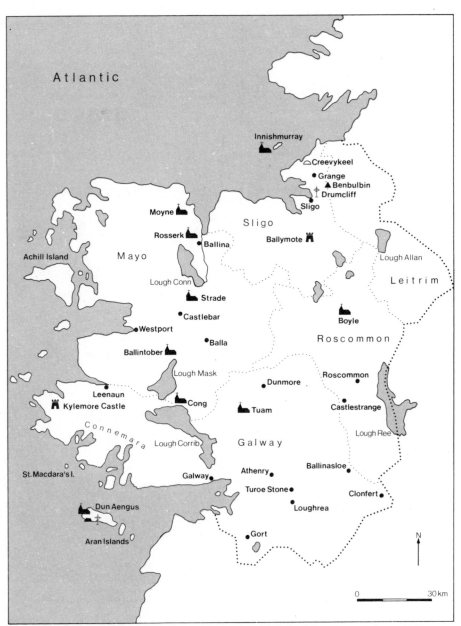

The province of Connacht, which includes the counties of Leitrim, Sligo, Mayo, Galway, and Roscommon.

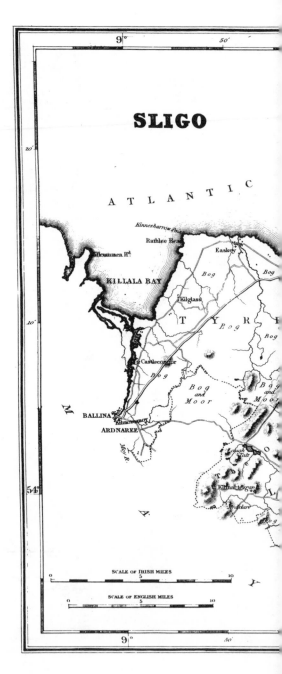

Map of Sligo from Samuel Lewis's atlas, 1837.

page 45). Unfortunately, since the island is uninhabited, there is no regular boat service to it. The Beach Hotel in Mullaghmore will arrange a crossing.

A tall, wide stone wall broken by five gateways forms an oval barricade that is somewhat narrower at one end. The space inside this wall is divided into four sections, each with its own church and a number of beehive monks' huts. The largest space encloses the Teampull na Fhear (Church of the Men), which, with its stepped back roof and flush door, typifies the very earliest Irish church structures. The northwest corner is reserved for the Teach Molaise, a primitively designed building ascribed to St. Molaise, who founded the cloister in the sixth century. Numbers of ornamented gravestones and cross fragments surround both the Teampull na Teinidh (Church of Fire) and the Teampull na mBan (Church of the Women), which stands outside the wall.

One peculiarity of this site is the presence of three altars along the road, all of which are decorated with crosses. The churches were small, a bit over 30 feet long at the most, and they could not contain all of the monks. So when the weather permitted, masses were held in the open air. On Inishmurray, there also used to be several curse stones; circling them a number of times while praying ensured that a specified person would suffer one's wrath.

There is a true story from the time of Inishmurray's heyday. St. Finian was known for his beautifully illuminated manuscripts, and he guarded them jealously. St. Columba, famous for being an experienced and quite rapid scribe, paid a visit to St. Finian. During the night, he crept into the church in order to copy St. Finian's psalter by candlelight. For hours the saint worked, quickly tracing letter after letter in the minuscule script that served the spread of Christianity so well. The head of the cloister was not long in discovering the deed, and he complained to the king of Sligo, who declared that the copy is to the book as a calf is to its mother cow. St. Columba refused to accept this judgment, ultimately leading to a fierce battle at Culdreimne, at the foot of Ben Bulben, in 561, in which some 3,000 men were slain. St. Columba was victorious, but he could not rest easy in light of these terrible sacrifices, and full of remorse he abandoned his homeland.

Not far from the battlefield stands another foundation of this saint's, *Drumcliff*, which is interesting primarily for its cross and the grave of William Butler Yeats. The poet wished to be buried in this region, which he loved and often wrote about, and he composed his own epitaph. His grave lies directly next to the entrance to the church. Near the road, the stump of a burned round tower marks the entrance of the cemetery. According to local legend, it will collapse on top of the wisest man who passes by it. Next to the short trail to the church, there is a high cross from the tenth century. Its ring is less important than those of earlier crosses, and its reliefs, less rigidly divided, show a transition to the final stage of the high cross (illus. 55, page 120). The east side shows Adam and Eve, Cain, Daniel, and the Crucifixion; the west side, the circumcision of Christ, the Crucifixion, and unidentifiable scenes, as well as ornamentation.

The county town of *Sligo*, bustling by day, grows very quiet in the evening. Dinnertime here, as in Ireland generally, is quite early. The setting sun fades in the waters of Sligo Bay, which cuts deep into the coastline and is protected by Coney Island at its mouth.

Sligo's Dominican abbey was built in 1252 by Maurice FitzGerald, the baron of Offaly

Nave and choir of Sligo abbey.

Sligo City Hall.

and founder of the town. The greater part of this often destroyed establishment dates from the fifteenth century; its choir, with vertically divided lancet windows and richly ornamented tombs, probably goes back to the thirteenth century. The cloister, which boasts ornamented double columns, is well worth seeing. Like the chancel and the tower, the east window belongs to the later period of building. On the north wall of the nave is the tomb of Cormac O'Crean with depictions of the Crucifixion, Mary and John, and a number of saints. Every August, the lectures of the International Yeats Summer School are held here. Other points of interest in Sligo are St. John's Cathedral, the cathedral, the city hall, and the historical museum.

The road to Ballina leads past *Ballymote Castle*. This fortress, built in 1300 by Richard de Burgh, was the strongest in Connacht; its ruins are flanked by hexagonal towers. The road then heads toward the Ox Mountains, which loom like a barrier.

From either Sligo or Ballymote, it is worthwhile taking a brief side trip to the south to visit the Cistercian abbey of Boyle in County Roscommon (see p. 212).

Mayo

Rosserk Abbey—Moyne Abbey —Errew Abbey—Strade Abbey —Ballintober Abbey—Croagh Patrick—Cong Abbey—Ross Abbey (Galway)

Mountains, boats, beaches, and cliffs offer endless opportunity for recreation in County Mayo. Achill Island, now connected by a bridge to the mainland, is especially popular with tourists. Along the shores of this county, boats set off in pursuit of blue sharks and other deep-sea fish. But there are also a number of abbeys and churches to visit.

North of Ballina, two abbeys testify to the strength of the Franciscan order. *Rosserk Abbey*, reached by a narrow path across the fields, dates, like nearby Moyne Abbey, from the fifteenth century. A Romanesque doorway leads into a single-nave church with a splendid west window that goes back to the first stage of construction, as does the window of the southern chapel. On one of the columns in the piscina there is a rare depiction of a round tower. The abbey's house-keeping buildings, including fireplaces on the second story, are well preserved.

In *Moyne Abbey*, likewise built close to the water, a chapel adjacent to the nave gives the church a spaciousness that Rosserk lacks. It had cloisters on the north, a chapter house and refectory, and housekeeping buildings of all kinds; its size was common in Western monasteries. Moyne Friary was founded by MacWilliam Burke in 1460 on orders from Pope Nicholas. The arched entryway and tower date from the seventeenth century. The tower steps are somewhat derelict.

After a short side trip to Rathfran, a Dominican settlement from the middle of the twelfth century, the road leads southward to Lough Conn, which is divided in half by a spit of land. At the tip of this spit lies *Errew Abbey*, an Augustinian cloister with remarkable three-part windows and a baptismal font. Not far from Errew, there is a small, rectangular oratory called Templenagalliaghdoo (Church of the Black Nun). The oldest foundation at this spot was St. Tighernan's in the sixth century. The present entrance

Moyne Abbey.

Ground plan of Moyne Abbey.

1. Nave
2. Tower
3. Choir
4. Transept
5. Chapels
6. Sacristy
7. Cloister garden
8. Storerooms
9. Chapter house
10. Kitchen
11. Refectory
12. Dormitory

on the south side and the anteroom on the north may well have been added during reconstruction.

County Mayo's varied landscape provides constant delights, and as one drives farther south it becomes increasingly colorful and fertile. At Foxford, which is a mecca for fishermen, the Franciscans built *Strade Abbey* 600 years ago. Six slender windows admit light into the church, which contains a lovely tomb with a gallery of reliefs. These figures appear to be protecting the sleep of the deceased and attesting to his faith. Three kings, Christ showing his wounds, a kneeling man (perhaps representing the artist), a bishop with his hand raised in admonition, and Sts. Peter and Paul are all lined up in a row. On another tomb near the east window two more kneeling men, quite conscious of their own dignity, flank the Pietà.

Ballintober Abbey, which lies still farther south, was founded by a member of the O'Connor family in about 1216. The structure was renovated only recently, and it now constitutes a kind of compromise between a place of worship and a monument. The interplay between the original and the restored portions is delightful. St. Patrick had established a monastery on this spot before setting off to fast on the mountain named after him, but nothing of it remains. The cruciform foundation walls and the windows survived the devastation of Cromwell quite well, although most of the churches of County Mayo suffered the same ravaging as those in the rest of Ireland.

From the partially preserved cloisters, in good weather, one can look up and see the quartzite cone of *Croagh Patrick*, Ireland's holy mountain, which rises above the south coast of Clew Bay. Here, the patron saint fasted like Christ in the wilderness until, according to legend, he acquired the strength to save an infinite number of souls. Each year on Lughnorad (Garland Sunday, the last Sunday in July), the Celtic summer festival, tens of thousands of pilgrims gather at Murrisk Abbey on Clew Bay. At night, they then make the difficult climb up the narrow trail to celebrate at the remains of Temple Patrick.

Cong Abbey is the highlight of any tour through Mayo (illus. 98, page 192). Irish Romanesque architecture is nowhere so well preserved as here. The Romanesque doorway, on the north face, is embellished with beautiful sculptures, some of which, along various capitals in the cloisters, were tastefully restored in the nineteenth century. The doorway to the chapter house is also splendidly detailed.

Some 9 miles southeast of Cong, over the border into Galway, is the impressive ruin of the Franciscan cloister of *Ross (or Rosserrily) Abbey* at Headford, founded in 1351 (illus. 79, page 181).

In Ballinrobe, north of Cong, a particularly severe landlord, Captain Boycott, was driven to despair by the passive resistance of the Irish. Thus the term "boycott" was born.

Galway and Roscommon

Connemara—Clifden— Galway—Aran Islands— Dún Aengus—Tuam

Fish-filled Lough Corrib divides Galway into two completely different regions. To the west of the lake the coastal mountains thrust up, while to the east the limestone plain that extends across almost all of Ireland begins. The territory west of the lake is known as *Connemara* (illus. 1, 60, 61, 107, 118, pages 33, 122, 228, 233). Scarcely anywhere else do so many types of landscape produce such a variety of charming views. Quartzite mountain ranges are garlanded by brilliant rhododendrons, and sheer cliffs brace themselves against the sea. In the northwest, an elongated fjord separates Galway from Mayo. The road leads along it to *Clifden*, a small village that hosts the famous Connemara Pony Show annually at the end of August, where both tourists and natives assemble. Along with the peninsulas of Kerry, Connemara belongs to the *Gaeltacht*, the region in which Irish is the first language and Irish traditions live on. Only here

A 19th-century view of Clifden.

A 19th-century view of a street in Galway.

tection of their patron saint on St. MacDara.

The route proceeds without interruption toward the county seat, *Galway*, on Galway Bay. In the early Middle Ages, Galway had an active trade with Spain, and a number of patrician houses with Renaissance façades testify to the city's former ties to the Continent. Galway numbers some 30,000 inhabitants, and it is the intellectual and cultural center of the Gaelic west; its university, founded in 1908, specializes in Gaelic language and literature. At the St. Nicholas Church, which was built in 1320, a plaque commemorates the story of the mayor of Galway, James Lynch, who condemned his own son to death for the murder of a host. The citizenry grumbled about the inhuman sentence, hoping instead to see the murder punished with a fine of money, which was more consistent with Celtic tradition. But the mayor remained firm, and since no one would carry out the sentence, he put his son to death himself by hanging him from the balcony of his

are the old customs, like wakes, ceilys (dances), and matchmaking still practiced.

Kylemore Castle, on the lake of the same name, north of Clifden, is well worth visiting. And visitors should take a side trip into southern Connemara. Just before Glendollagh Lake, a right turn off the T71 onto the L102 brings one to a stretch of coastline with mostly cliffs. Past Bertraghboy Bay one comes to Carna, where it is possible to rent a boat and go out to St. MacDara's Island to visit the early Christian stone church founded by that saint in the sixth century. This structure, patterned after earlier wooden churches, has a low entryway, a steep roof, and a lovely round-arch window. On the saint's feast days (June 16 and September 28), pilgrims converge here from all over Ireland. Seamen, especially, beg the pro-

A 19th-century view of an arch in the Claddagh, Galway.

James Lynch's house as it looked in 1879.

house. He never left the house again. Today, the building is occupied by the Munster and Leinster Bank (illus. 117, page 232).

Ships depart almost daily from Galway for the *Aran Islands*, which also belong to the Gaeltacht and whose isolation has enabled a number of older customs to be preserved. The old Gaelic character and the historical monuments of the Aran Islands pervade the works of Liam O'Flaherty and John Millington Synge.

Of the many churches, crosses, gravestones, slabs with incised drawings, and dolmens that survive on the islands of Inishmore, Inishmaan, and Inisheer (illus. 101–103, page 226), only the most important ones that might be seen on a one-day tour will be described. The Firbolgs were likely the earliest inhabitants of the Aran Islands. After being defeated by the Tuatha dé Danaan in the battle at Moytura, and finding themselves unable to raise the unbearably high taxes imposed by the king of Tara, Cairbre Nia Fer (first century A.D.), they established a new home for themselves here.

This people fortified the islands and chose its own leaders, of whom Aengus is immortalized by the massive fort that bears his name. In about 490 A.D., St. Enda founded a cloister near Killeany that would become the place where many saints were schooled, among them St. Ciaran and St. Finian. Since they were frequently unable to count on getting supplies from the mainland, the islanders produced almost everything themselves. Today, they make their living from tourism and lobster fishing, which is quite lucrative.

Dún Aengus, the huge prehistoric ring fort on Inishmore, is built close to the 300-foot cliffs and is the most extensive fortification in Western Europe (illus. 66, page 125). Three semicircular stone walls

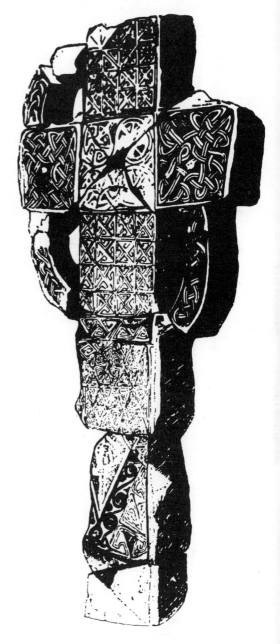

Cross near Temple Brecan, Aran Islands.

209

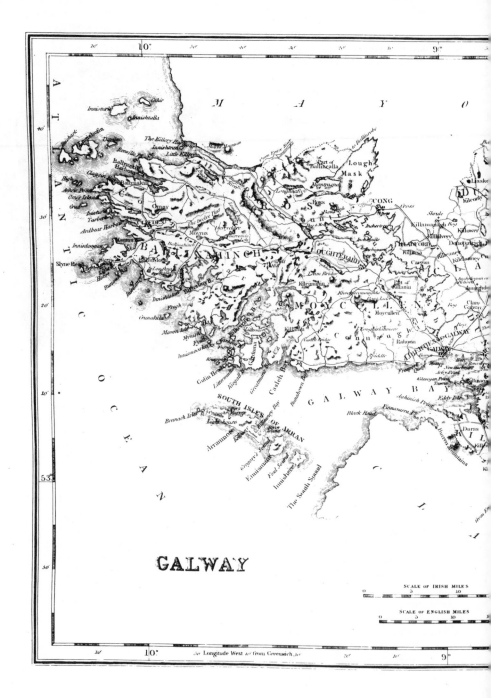

GALWAY

SCALE OF IRISH MILES

SCALE OF ENGLISH MILES

Map of Galway from Samuel Lewis's atlas, 1837.

Tuam Cathedral.

protect the spot. The innermost wall is fitted out with corridors and chambers. One still does not know why such a massive fortress was constructed on the island; perhaps the Aran Islands were once connected to the mainland by a narrow strip of land that later sank into the sea. Around the three stone walls there are thousands of upright stone blocks that serve as a further protective barrier.

On Inishmaan there are dolmens that, according to legend, once served as shelters for Dairmaid and Gráinne.

If one proceeds directly northward from Meath, one can now drive from Galway into the interior of Ireland to Clonmacnoise in order to experience something of the Shan-

non Plain. Along the way, there are a number of art treasures worth seeing. Simply driving about without a plan is even rewarding here. Heading northward, the first stop is *Tuam*, whose founder, St. Iarlath, was a pupil at the monastery founded by St. Enda on Inishmore. The present-day cathedral was erected after a fire in the eighteenth century, but the Romanesque nave and choir from the twelfth century were saved. On the shaft of a high cross one can see a prayer for King Turloch O'Connor. Another cross stands in the middle of town.

A short way past Dunmore (castle and Augustinian monastery) one crosses into the next county, Roscommon.

Roscommon (Roscommon)— Boyle Abbey (Roscommon) —Clonfert (Galway)—Turoe Stone (Galway)—Athenry (Galway)—Kilmacduagh (Galway)

The town of *Roscommon* boasts a thirteenth-century square castle fortified with round

towers at the corners, one of the largest in the British Isles (illus. 112, page 230). In the north of County Roscommon, near the Sligo border, lies *Boyle Abbey* (illus. 110, page 230). It takes less time to reach this abbey from Sligo (Ballinafad) than from the south; be warned, though, that the church may be locked. The well-preserved ruins of this Cistercian abbey, notably its church and its guest house, stand right beside the River Boyle. It was founded by Maurice O'Duffy in 1148 as a branch of Mellifont. In 1235, it was heavily damaged, and it was dissolved by Cromwell in 1569. The long church nave is remarkable for its Early Gothic arches on the north side and Romanesque ones on the south. The capitals of the columns are splendidly worked. The windows in the transept are roughly 200 years younger. To get to the decorative La Tène stone of Castlestrange, drive southwest from Roscommon on the T15 to Athleague; then take the L135 to Castlestrange. Here, there is a marked turnoff onto a private road.

From Roscommon the road leads southward past Lough Ree to Athlone, Clonmacnoise, and *Clonfert* (from the Gaelic *cluain fhearta*, or "field of graves"), a foundation of St. Brendan's from about 560 that preserves the most beautiful Romanesque church doorway in Ireland (illus. 94 and 95, pages 190 and 191). There is scarcely anything comparable to it anywhere else in the British Isles.

On either side of the doorway there are five offset pilasters that lean slightly toward the center and are variously decorated. They are executed in the manner familiar from French cathedrals except that there is no tympanum. The arches above the columns, each forming a perfect semicircle, are richly ornamented with stylized plant and animal motifs as well as interwoven and filigree designs. The capitals are simple Romanesque cubes on which there are grotesque, almost whimsical animal heads of various sizes. A narrow, triangular gable reveals Mediterranean influences, and in the lower part of it there are six smaller pilasters with round arches in which are set human heads that reveal clearly recognizable, individualized

Representations of animals in the Urnes style from the Clonfert portal, Galway.

features, probably deriving from Celtic tradition. It is still uncertain just what these faces may signify; it is conceivable that they represent a succession of especially notable monks and abbots. Smaller triangles fill the upper portion of the gable. These are decorated with rosette-shaped leaves and blossoms; in the spaces between them are more markedly individualized heads. Only the north transept of the church itself is fully preserved.

A few miles north of Loughrea, near Bullaun, is the *Turoe Stone*, the most beautiful relic from the La Tène period (third to second centuries B.C.) in Ireland. One finds it by driving through Bullaun and turning to the left at the end of town. The round, evenly worked block, ornamented with plant designs, probably served some ritual function (illus. 10, page 37).

Near *Athenry*, a twelfth-century lord built a castle (open Monday through Friday, 8:00A.M.–5:00P.M.) and an abbey for the Dominicans, which sometime later served briefly as a university. After passing through Clarinbridge and Gort, one comes to the last stop in Connacht, *Kilmacduagh*, a monastic settlement with churches and a slanting tower, roughly 115 feet high, that stands next to an eleventh-century cathedral (illus. 72, page 177).

MUNSTER

Nowhere else is the adjective "emerald" so appropriate as in the southwest of Ireland. Its proximity to the Gulf Stream and prevailing mild southwesterly winds give the landscape a subtropical character, with a wealth and variety of vegetation quite unusual for this latitude. Like great, long fingers, a series of peninsulas reaches out into the Atlantic. Munster receives more tourists than any other part of Ireland. American and English visitors especially favor it.

Clare

Corcomroe Abbey—Poulnabrone Dolmens—Cliffs of Moher —Kilfenora—Dysert O'Dea —Ennis—Bunratty Castle

Between Galway Bay and Shannon Mouth, bordered on the east by the Shannon River and Lough Derg—not to be confused with the small lake in Donegal—the sea breaks against the massive cliffs of Clare.

Near small Poulnaclogh Bay, off Galway Bay, *Corcomroe Abbey* stands in a charming, isolated valley. The pious king Donal Mor O'Brien is said to have founded the abbey in 1194. Corcomroe Abbey has two transepts, each with a chapel built onto it. The capitals in the choir are ornamented with lotus vines. The austere influence of the Irish Romanesque is visible in the lovely roof of the choir. The tomb of one of the patrons of the monastery, Conor na Siudaine O'Brien, buried in 1267, stands in a niche on the north wall.

Somewhat farther west, after Ballyvaghan, the L51 branches off to the south, bringing one to the *Poulnabrone Dolmens* (illus. 7, page 36). These lie a bit off the road in the middle of a barren waste of rocky cliffs known as The Burren. This side trip can also be made from Kilfenora, but the coast road is prettier.

The coast route leads past Lisdoonvarna, a spa known for its waters, rich in iron and sulfur. One soon arrives at the wild, 650-foot *Cliffs of Moher* (illus. 119, page 234). The sea gulls can be seen flying far below. From the parking area, one can climb up to O'Brien's Tower, which provides the best panorama of the series of imposing cliffs. Only a few miles to the south, there are again broad, sandy beaches.

Inland, farther to the east, stands the cathedral of *Kilfenora*. It is estimated to be about 700 years old and has some Early Gothic windows and striking capitals, although not to be compared with the elegance and delicacy of those at Jerpoint Abbey.

In addition to a number of cross fragments in the cemetery, the twelfth-century Doorty Cross is particularly noteworthy here (illus. 58, page 121). This blocky cross approaches the simpler standing stones in form and rests on a wide, flat slab. The cross ring is set back and unperforated. Only a few crudely worked low-relief figures ornament the front and back. One side contains a crucifix with a galloping horseman beneath it; from his head, an ornamental band issues in the Urnes style. The other side is divided into three compartments. In the bottom third, one can make out a bird of prey and its victim; in the middle, two figures, each with a staff; and on top, a bishop with mitre—his left hand holds a crozier and his right hand with its extended fingers seems to gesture a benediction.

Outside the cemetery stands the West Cross, from the late eleventh or early twelfth century. This cross, with a tall shaft and small circle, once had a base, but it has been lost through the course of the centuries. With the exception of the figure of the crucified Christ, almost the entire surface is covered with ornamentation.

On the way to Dysert O'Dea and the best-preserved cross of the late period, one passes a church ruin at Killinaboy that has a *sheila na gig* (*sheila* is the Gaelic equivalent of "Julia," *gig* means "nipple") over its doorway. This is a depiction of a grotesque, naked female figure with exaggerated sexual attributes and was a fertility idol. Apart from adorning the outside of churches, such figures are found only above the doorways of castles.

The precinct of *Dysert O'Dea* consists of the stump of a round tower and a church ruin, with windows, from the end of the thirteenth century, and a portal—without gable—from the twelfth century. The outermost arch of the four-part portal has a number of grotesque animal heads as well as human faces marked by an overpowering

fate; in spite of the abstract representation, one can clearly discern their sorrow and bitterness along with meditative and fatalistic features.

The cross of Dysert O'Dea (illus. 56 and 57, page 121) resembles the one at Kilfenora, but it has fewer figures. There is no ring on this twelfth-century limestone cross, and the crossarms are short and wide. The ornaments and the relief of Daniel in the lion's den on the back suggest Scandinavian influence in the form of the Ringerike style. The two figures on the west side stand out in high relief. A bishop with a crook fills the lower half; above him, there is a figure of Christ with arms outstretched. Their faces are animated, not monotonously stylized as on Bible crosses. The cross of Dysert O'Dea reveals what is lacking in all of the older sculpture: here, the human beings are not treated as mere actors in some arbitrary event, but as distinct personalities. One can thus detect an approach toward the artistic sensibility of the Continent.

Not far from Dysert O'Dea, southward along the road to Limerick, lies *Ennis*, whose friary is well preserved by Irish standards (illus. 92 and 93, page 190). Donough Cairbreach O'Brien, a king of Thomond (present-day County Clare), permitted a few Franciscans to found the settlement in 1241; its initial form is today suggested only by

LEFT: *Daniel in the lions' den, from the Dysert O'Dea cross.* ABOVE: *detail from the Dysert O'Dea portal.*

215

Galway Bay

Dun Aengus

Corcomroe Abbey

Aran Islands

Poulnabrone

Lorrh

Cliffs of Moher

Kilfenora

Liscannor

Dysert O'Dea

Lough Derg

A t l a n t i c

Ennistymone

Nenagh

Ennis

Clare

Clare

Quin

Killaloe

Bunratty Castle

Limerick

Kilkee

Shannon Mouth

Askeaton

Adare

LoughGur

Listowel

Ardagh

Limerick

Tipp

Ardfert

B

Tralee

Kerry

Cork

Kilmalkedar

Gallarus Oratory

Caherconree

Lis

Ballyferriter

Dingle

Dunquin

Ventry

Ballintaggart

Mallow

Dunbeg

Dingle

Killorglin

Aghadoe

Dingle Bay

Innisfallen

Killarney

Lough Leane

Gap of
Dunloe

Muckross Abbey

Iveragh

Blarney Castle

Cork

Kenmare

River Lee

Cloy

Skellig Rocks

Staigue Fort

Kilcrea

Kenmare River

Beara

Glengariff

Kinsale

Castletown Bere

Dunboy Castle

Bantry Bay

Bantry House

Drombeg

216

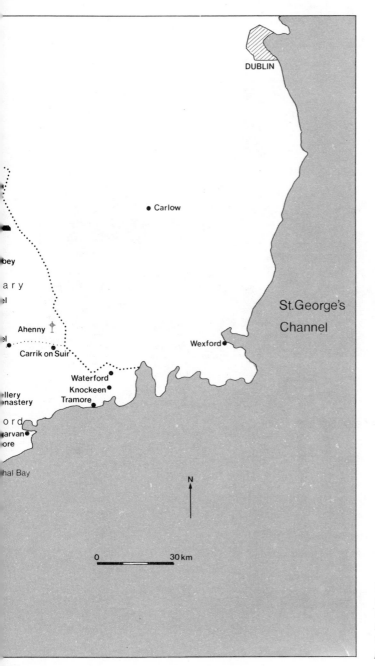

The province of Munster, which includes the counties of Clare, Limerick, Kerry, Cork, Waterford, and Tipperary.

Quin Abbey.

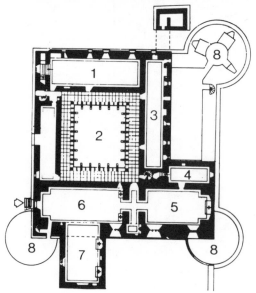

Ground plan of Quin Abbey.
1. *Refectory*
2. *Cloister garden*
3. *Kitchen*
4. *Sacristy*
5. *Altar nave*
6. *Nave*
7. *Transept*
8. *Bastions*

Bunratty Castle.

the choir and the east window. Six hundred years ago, Ennis accommodated 350 monks and more than 600 pupils and was considered the most important educational institution for the clergy and the upper class. The main portions of the church nave survive from that time, as do the west portal and the windows in the south transept. Visitors are most attracted to the tomb of MacMahon (died 1475). Late Gothic embellishments, both the carved figures and the ornamentation, have been mastered to perfection here. After careful restoration, Ennis once again came into the possession of the Franciscans, who also own Quin Abbey (illus. 82, page 182), somewhat farther east. Powerful bastions give this cloister a fortresslike appearance, but *Bunratty Castle* beckons. This imposing seat preserves its original interiors to a great extent. The

enterprising owner of the castle hosts two medieval banquets daily from April to October, extravagant affairs especially popular with tourists from the neighboring luxury hotels.

Those who are willing to take a detour can visit St. Flannan's Oratory, which was built in 1182 at *Killaloe*, a beautifully situated spot at the southern tip of Lough Derg. Its richly ornamented portal is a masterpiece of the Irish Romanesque style. Also of interest here is Thorgrim's Stone, a granite stone that is unique for being incised with two quite different scripts—runes and Ogham inscriptions. The more direct route, however, leads to the next county, and one can also visit Killaloe by driving upstream along the Shannon out of Limerick.

Limerick

Limerick—Desmond Castle— Adare—Ardagh (Longford)— Lough Gur

This county, one of the few regions in Ireland where grain can be grown, presents a landscape of fields and hedges, ideal for autumn hunts. (To take part in these events, one must know their private sponsors, generally local landowners; riding clubs rarely schedule them.) Limerick also has about 400 castle ruins, so one can easily make one's own discoveries.

The city of *Limerick* (from *Luimneach*,

A 19th-century view of Limerick.

King John's Castle.

meaning "bleak place") is an ambitious industrial center today. It is perhaps best known for the popular five-line doggerel verse form that shares its name; actually, the origins of the limerick are unclear, but it probably comes from England. Danish Vikings founded this strategically important fortification 1,000 years ago, and the city walls are still partially preserved. King John's Castle (illus. 115, page 232), which stands directly above the Shannon, changed hands a number of times before being destroyed once and for all 300 years ago.

Limerick is also known as the "city of the broken treaty": in 1691, it was forced to surrender to a large army of William of Orange, and the Irish responded to English claims to dominion with large-scale emigration. Guarantees of confessional freedom for the Catholics and the inviolability of ownership of property were not respected, and three-quarters of the land came into English hands. On the west side of Thomond's Bridge, one can still see the stone on which the treaty was presumably signed.

The choir stalls in St. Mary's Cathedral are remarkable; they are carved of black oak and ornamented with charming animals and fabulous beasts. Portions of the church, the nave and doorway, date from 1180 to 1190, when it was built by Donal Mor O'Brien. In the fifteenth century, several chapels were added, as were a number of tombs—including that of Donat O'Brien, the great earl of Thomond. The bell tower was built later; it is well worth climbing up to admire the bells, dated 1678.

The ruins of *Desmond Castle* (1199) stand on an island in the River Deel in Askeaton. Only the large hall is well preserved. This castle was a refuge for the last earl of Desmond after his revolt against Ormond failed.

Adare (from *ath dara*, meaning "ford of the oaks") resembles an English country town. Its well-kept houses and gardens are laid out in the English manner, and its residents have adapted their way of life to the British model. The highlight of the town is the park of the earl of Dunraven: the River Maigue flows through it, and it contains various interesting structures, particularly an old castle with semicircular fortified towers. Adare Manor, built in the neo-Gothic style, has nicely preserved interiors. It also houses an impressive collection of art, including paintings by Canaletto, Ruysdael, and Reynolds as well as Chinese and Japanese inlays and paintings on wall chests and vases.

Next to the river, there is a small abbey

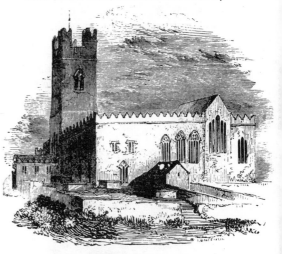

St. Mary's Cathedral.

Depictions of animals from the choirstalls of St. Mary's Cathedral.

221

that was once reached by way of Kilmallock Gate, a ruin standing not far from the cloister. An earl of Kildare presented the newly built church to the Franciscan order in 1464. The nave, the transept, and the small chapels survive from the time of its construction, whereas the backless seats for the celebrants and the windows date from a later period. Its cloisters contain flat arches, each of which spans three smaller and beautifully carved arcades, a most uncommon design. A small stone bridge with several arches crosses the river here. When one stands on it, one can look back at these ruins in the midst of a magical, almost primeval, garden landscape.

At *Ardagh*, the next stop, archeologists discovered the Ardagh Chalice (illus. 22 and 23, pages 41 and 42) and a brooch in 1868. Both of these priceless treasures are now in the National Museum in Dublin.

Anyone interested in prehistory will want to explore the area surrounding *Lough Gur*, a horseshoe-shaped lake in the eastern part of Limerick, close to the Tipperary border. Extensive excavations here have uncovered the earliest forms of houses yet discovered in Ireland and show that the region was inhabited continuously from the Neolithic period until the seventeenth century. Around the shores of the lake there are countless stones, dolmens, passage graves, menhirs, and foundations of various buildings, making Lough Gur a unique attraction. To the west of the lake, on the road from Kilmallock to Limerick, there is a stone circle where excavations have unearthed Bronze Age vessels and ceramics.

Kerry

Ardfert—Dingle Peninsula (Caherconree—Ballintaggart —Dingle—Oratory of Gallarus —Kilmalkedar—Dunquin— Fahan—Dunbeg)—Gap of Dunloe—Upper Lough Leane —Lough Leane—Aghadoe— Killarney—Innisfallen— Muckross Abbey—Ring of Kerry —Killorglin—Skellig Michael —Staigue Fort

Adfert Abbey.

This popular county is an ideal place for those interested in either the natural sciences or Gaelic culture, which lives on here. The three peninsulas, Dingle, Iveragh, and Beara, whose roadways are among the most beautiful in the world, are nearly as crowded with visitors as the district of Killarney, with its lakes and deep chasms, which is one of the favored tourist areas in Ireland. It is recommended that one schedule a vacation in the area before the peak tourist season

Tomb in Adfert Abbey.

(illus. 63, 122, 123, pages 123, 236, 237).

The first stop in Kerry is *Ardfert*, near Tralee, a foundation of St. Brendan's. Nothing survives to mark the saint's first church, but it was similar to the Oratory of Gallarus, on the Dingle Peninsula. The oldest part of the cathedral, the Romanesque west portal from the twelfth century, permits one to view the interior. The blind arcades date from the same period, and shortly afterward, Ardfert assumed its present form, with lancet windows. A smaller Romanesque church near the major structure is fascinating because of the simplicity and clarity of its form. A round tower collapsed here several hundred years ago in a heavy storm.

The *Dingle Peninsula* deserves at least one whole day. Experienced hikers may want to climb Ireland's second highest mountain, Mount Brandon (3,116 feet; roughly four hours round trip).

Slieve Mish marks the beginning of the peninsula; beyond it, one re-enters the Gaeltacht. Here, one is struck by the perseverance of the people and the durability of their monuments, among them standing stones and Ogham stones, churches, and forts. Archaic prototypes have been blended with Gaelic elements, and dating of these artifacts is generally difficult. Near the western peak of Slieve Mish, at about the 1,500-foot level, lies *Caherconree*, one of the few promontory forts in the interior of the country. The fort is hard to find, and the climb up to it is both strenuous and time-consuming; but one is rewarded for one's efforts by a splendid view and by the fort itself, with its 14-foot-thick and 350-foot-long stone wall. Caherconree plays a major role in the old saga of Cúchulainn.

Near *Ballintaggart*, on the south coast, there are some Ogham stones that display crosses, some of them swastikalike, next to the Gaelic inscriptions. Clearly, the first Christians added these symbols in an effort to check the power of the heathen spirits. Unfortunately it is impossible to decipher all the inscriptions, since a variety of scripts were used, but generally the stones bear a consistent message that invokes the name of the person buried beneath it.

Dingle is the westernmost town in Europe (except for a few island settlements). In its dockyards, small boats called *curraghs* (canoes) are made just like they were 3,000 years ago, when the first Stone Age inhabitants began producing the first devices for catching fish. These boats are made of tarred canvas—formerly animal skins were used—stretched across a wooden skeleton, and they are remarkably seaworthy (illus. 105 and 121, pages 227 and 235). It was in such a boat that St. Brendan set out to sea in search of the land of eternal youth (*Tir na nOg*). He never came back. Pre-Columbian Indian legends tell of a white god who performed good deeds roughly at the time of this saint, suggesting the possibility that St. Brendan reached America.

Today, Dingle appears as a peaceful fishing settlement. Its inhabitants go out to catch mackerel or to hunt seals. A superstition survives from the time of the Druids that the soul of an accursed man can enter into a seal. Thus, these fishermen are not entirely comfortable hunting seals even now. There always lurks the possibility that a leprechaun lies in wait to lure the sea hunter toward the deadly cliffs.

Near Milltown, a secondary road branches off toward Kilmalkedar. Just before this latter town, a sign directs one to the famous *Oratory of Gallarus* (illus. 71, page 128), a well-preserved early Christian chapel. This structure was almost unaffected by the forms of Roman architecture that influenced practically all of Europe. With its nearly square layout, 22 by 18 feet, it is a stone adaptation and elaboration of the early Irish churches made of wood and wattle; it is shaped like an overturned boat. Worked quarry stones with joints slanting outward have been overlapped with astonishing

precision, resulting in a vaulted interior that was probably finished in some sort of crude plaster. A row of capstones along the 16-foot-high ridge makes the whole structure weatherproof. All the stones of these mortarless walls fit as tightly today as they did when the building was first constructed roughly 1,200 to 1,300 years ago; aside from a slight sag in the line of the roof and in the upper third of the side walls, the church has survived unchanged. A narrow doorway, just high enough for a person to pass through it, leads beneath a horizontal lintel at the west gable end into the 10-by-15-foot interior. Two stones projecting inward above the lintel and with holes drilled in them must have secured a doorjamb. Except for a small semicircular window in the east gable that becomes larger toward the inside, there are no other openings in the structure. Near the oratory is an early Christian stone with an incised cross.

In *Kilmalkedar*, where St. Maolcethair directed a monastery in the seventh century, there is a chapel in the Romanesque style. Its design was surely derived from Cormac's Chapel in Cashel, which was the first building of this type in Ireland. Especially uncommon and novel was the tympanum, with a man's head and unidentifiable animal figures that resemble sculptures, in the choir. The exterior walls, as at Cashel, are embellished with blind arcades. The gable was apparently built after the model of wooden churches, less for structural reasons than to suit the architectural taste of the period. Inside are a number of stone blocks decorated with crosses and an alphabet stone.

Past Ballyferriter and Clogher Head, one comes to *Dunquin*, a mecca for all who are interested in Gaelic culture and folklore. On weekend evenings, the population of the whole area attends the local dances, which are held for the residents' own pleasure

100. Inisheer—farmsteads and castle ruins in a hostile landscape, Aran Islands. ▷

101–103. Inisheer—fishermen's houses, walls, and grazing plots. The stone walls serve as fencing and prevent wind erosion.

104. On the Aran Islands, the donkey is still the most important means of transport.

105. Fishermen on the Aran Islands have to row far out to make a good catch.

106. Market day in Ballina, Mayo.

107. Near Roundstone on Bertraghboy Bay, Connemara, Galway.

108. Farmhouses in Donegal.

109. One of the best-preserved round towers in Ireland (6th century), belonging to the monastic foundation
of St. Molaise on Devenish Island in Lough Erne, Fermanagh (Northern Ireland).

110. Cistercian monastery, c. 1150, Boyle,
Roscommon.

111. O'Connor tomb, Roscommon Abbey,
Roscommon.

112. Roscommon Castle—castle ruins with round fortification towers, 13th century.

113. Dunluce Castle, built about 1300 by Richard de Burgh, Antrim (Northern Ireland).

114. Tranarossan Bay, near Sheep Haven, Rosquill Peninsula, Donegal.

115. Limerick—view across the Shannon to Thurmond's Bridge and King John's Castle.

116. Donegal Castle. The castle of the O'Donnells, near the River Eask, stands in the middle of the town of Donegal.

117. Lynch's House, Galway.

120. Coastline near Slea Head, Dingle Peninsula, Kerry.

121. Irish Atlantic fishermen with their nimble boats, or *curraghs*.

119. The Cliffs of Moher, Clare, one of Europe's most magnificent coastlines. The cliffs are as high as 650 feet.

122. Ross Castle (16th century) near Killarney, Kerry.

123. Ring of Kerry. The famous coast road leads from Killorglin through Cahirciveen to Kenmare.

124, 125. River Liffey and O'Connell Bridge, Dublin

126–129. At 328 feet, Dublin's St. Patrick's Cathedral (1190) is the longest church structure in Ireland; College of Science; Trinity College; the Four Courts.

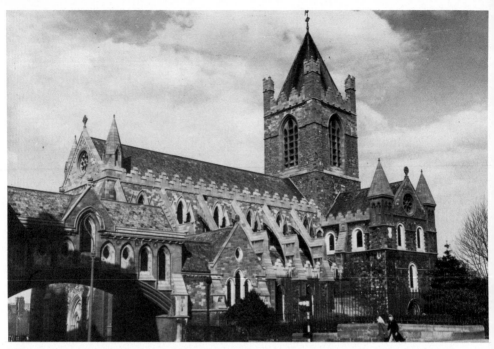

130, 131. Christ Church Cathedral, Dublin, was founded about 1038, rebuilt about 1170, and repeatedly enlarged and remodeled until the 19th century; Custom House on the River Liffey.

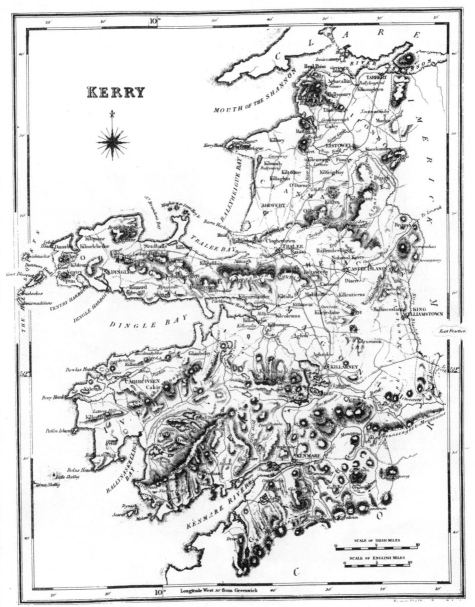

Map of Kerry from Samuel Lewis's atlas, 1837.

rather than to amuse tourists. One of the figure dances comes from the Blasket Islands, off the coast, which were inhabited until about twenty years ago. The primitive band, with bagpipe, fiddle, and flute, plays with great enthusiasm and touching dedication. The populace consists almost entirely of quite young people and the very old; the intervening generations have left to find work in the cities; local fishing has become unprofitable in these days of deep-sea fleets, and there are no other opportunities here. Although the great emigration of the nineteenth century is a thing of the past, the United States is still considered to be the land of unlimited opportunity.

Gap of Dunloe.

Between Slea Head (illus. 120, page 235) and *Fahan* quite a number of *clocháns* have survived. These are small, beehive-shaped stone huts constructed in the same manner as the Oratory of Gallarus. Even today, the inhabitants of Dingle build their storerooms and stalls according to these traditional methods. Many of the huts lack the top stones of their roofs, so one can easily see how they were built. Along the road near Fahan, there is an impressive collection of such structures. A few miles east of Slea Head, right out on the cliffs, invisible from the road and unmarked, is the promontory fort of *Dunbeg*. (When you see, on the land side of the road, an isolated, one-story house with *two* chimneys, stop the car and walk—along the edge of the fields, please—to the cliffs and to the fort. There is no path from the road to the fort. If you fail to find it, turn around at the first signpost of Ventry and drive back in the direction of Dunquin, exactly 3.5 miles.) Two walls of stone and earth protect it on the land side; on the ocean side, the cliffs ensure its impregnability. Originally the fort had walls with right angles, but during some restoration these corners were turned into curved ones. Inside, there are the remains of a house whose interior walls are round while the outer ones are squared; next to it, there are more beehive huts.

From the south coast of the Dingle Peninsula, one turns inland toward the region of Killarney. Just after Ballymalis Castle, the road branches off to the *Gap of Dunloe*, which reaches deep into Macgillycuddy's Reeks, Ireland's highest mountains (the highest summit is Carrantoohill, 3,404 feet). A few Ogham stones have been set up in a semicircle beside the road. Since such fine examples are rarely so accessible, one ought to see them before parking one's car at Kate

Kierney's inn and hiring a horse or a two-wheeled cart known as a "jaunting car." Or one can explore the Gap of Dunloe on foot. The lush green meadows contrast with the brown sandstone and the deep blue lakes. There is also a wide variety of vegetation, so the views are uncommonly colorful. St. Patrick is said to have banished all the snakes in Ireland to the last lake before the pass, Serpent Lake.

Those who have booked a one-day tour from Killarney at its Tourist Office now descend from the pass to *Upper Lough Leane* (illus. 63, page 123). From there, they embark on the boat ride through the lakes, connected by canals, to *Lough Leane* and back to Killarney. But those heading back toward Ballymalis Castle will pass by the church and round tower of *Aghadoe*, the remains of a monastery founded by St. Finian.

Doorway at Aghadoe monastery.

243

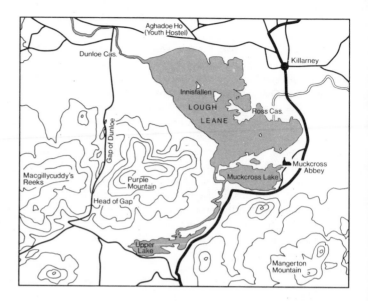

The district around Killarney.

Killarney (*cill airne*, or "blackthorn church") offers everything one would expect of a rather expensive tourist center; its large hotels and businesses cater to travelers. Killarney is an ideal spot from which to set out for all the attractions in the vicinity. The vacationer without a car should be advised that bus schedules frequently change, but the Tourist Office will gladly do what it can to give one up-to-date information. Here, one encounters horse-carts everywhere, and the coachmen are extremely friendly.

Anyone wishing to visit the island of *Innisfallen* will find boats available at Lough Leane. St. Finian founded a cloister on Innisfallen, as well as at Aghadoe. Around the end of the tenth century, Maelsuttain O'Carroll lived here; he was a famous physician and friend of the high king Brian Ború. A member of the O'Donoghue clan attacked the monastery in about 1200. (However, another O'Donoghue helped to

rebuild the cloister at Aghadoe.) Innisfallen rapidly recovered from this attack and became a center of culture and art. It was here that the Annals of Innisfallen, an important historical manuscript, were written in about 1215. A century later, the cloister adopted the rules of the Benedictine order. Near the shore, there is an oratory with a window on its east side and a semicircular Romanesque doorway.

On the east shore of Muckross Lake, which runs directly into Lough Leane, *Muckross Abbey* stands in the middle of Bourne-Vincent Memorial Park, another spot that is pleasant to visit by horse-drawn carriage. This well-preserved cloister, built some 500 years ago, lies surrounded by yew and ash trees. As at all Franciscan churches, its large tower was added later; this one is unique in Ireland in that it extends the full width of the nave. Structural differences on the various sides of the cloisters reveal a succession of building phases.

To the west of the lake rise Macgillicuddy's Reeks. This mountain mass dominates the approach to the Iveragh Peninsula, which can thus be reached only along the coast. The famous coast road, the *Ring of Kerry*, is fully comparable to the most beautiful drives on the Continent (illus. 123, page 237). The tourist who is not going out to the Skellig Rocks will still need a whole day for the trip around Iveragh Peninsula. The journey begins at *Killorglin* ("Church of Orglin"), whose annual Puck Fair, beginning on August 10 and running for three days, is famous far and wide. During this celebration, a crowned billy goat presides over the colorful event as the "king" of Killorglin.

After passing Lough Caragh, an angler's paradise, and a varied drive, one arrives either at the village of Cahirciveen or at Valentia Island. In summer, ships sail daily from Knightstown, on Valentia Island, to *Skellig Michael* (leaving at 10:00 A.M., only when the sea is calm), a craggy island roughly 10 miles off the coast. Seals sun themselves on the projecting rocks and swarms of sea-birds circle the cliffs. When arriving on Skellig Michael, one should ask the precise time of return, for there are no overnight accommodations. On this high, lonely spot, the patron saint of which is St. Michael, men devoted themselves for years to unlocking the secrets of nature. Europe has a number of sites dedicated to this saint: Monte Sant'Angelo in Italy, Mont Saint-Michel in France, St. Michael's Mount in Cornwall, and, the westernmost of them, this tiny island off the coast of Ireland. In spite of their remoteness from one another, they are all closely related because similar goals and studies were pursued on them. In Celtic times, the Druids studied the movement of the stars here, and the island's isolation and its hostile environment early attracted hermits to the island. For more than 100 years, the only inhabitants, though, have been the keepers of the lighthouse; their lives are quite difficult. The climb up the 650-foot cliffs is strenuous and adventuresome.

The early Christian monastery here resembles that of Kilmalkedar. It was founded by St. Finian, who established Innisfallen and other cloisters as well. A mere twenty graves survive from those inhabitants; the rigors of life led to the dissolution of the cloister in the twelfth century, when the monks moved to Ballinskelligs, on the mainland, and left behind the things they could not carry. Round *clocháns* (beehive huts) (illus. 15 and 16, page 39), with right-angled interior walls and shelves for foodstuffs, press together in the small level space that the monks created by laboriously cutting into the rock cliff and securing the earth behind retaining walls. A 650-foot-deep well ensured them fresh water, and steps carved into the rock made it possible to transport goods. Close to the monks' quarters, there is a small oratory resembling the Oratory of Gallarus on the Dingle Peninsula, described above.

Beginish, the small island north of Valentia Island, can be reached on foot at ebb tide. A stone above the doorway of a half-sunken stone house bears one of the few runic inscriptions in Ireland. It reads: "Lir set up this stone, M——— chiseled the runes."

On the south coast of Iveragh, it is well worth stopping at *Staigue Fort* (illus. 67, page 125)—turn inland at Castle Cove— which stands above the elongated bay of the Kenmare River. This Iron Age ring fort is 100 feet in diameter. Though less dramatic than Grianán of Aileach in Donegal, it is interesting nonetheless. A narrow corridor leads inside the wall, where staircases take one to the top of it. The road to Kenmare

Staigue Fort.

winds along the Kenmare River, where the grim farmhouses attest to the hard living conditions in these parts.

Beara, a third peninsula, belongs partly to Kerry and partly to Cork. It is best to approach this area from Glengariff, which lies on a side arm of Bantry Bay, several miles into County Cork.

Cork

Glengariff—Drombeg—Kinsale —Cork—Blarney Castle—Cloyne —Youghal

The largest county in Ireland comprises the southwesternmost section of the island. Its terrain is characterized by long, but not very high, ridges of mountains. In the warmer areas influenced by the Gulf Stream, a lush Mediterranean vegetation causes one to forget how far north one is. On the generally flat bays of the south coast lie the harbor towns of Cork, Kinsale, and Youghal. The flat beaches here virtually invited conquest, and thus it was the Vikings who founded most of these settlements.

Glengariff (*gleann garbh*, or "rugged canyon"), on the north shore of Bantry Bay, lies in a beautiful landscape and offers comfortable accommodations. Countless pubs will provide for "a good pint and a good sing-song." In this region, which belongs to the Gaeltacht, a number of uniquely Gaelic traditions have survived, especially folk music. ·

Among the more scenic spots in the immediate vicinity of Glengariff are Garinish Island, in the harbor, and nearby Barlay Lake. Near Castletownbere on Beara (also called Caha), shafts from ancient copper mines lead underground. Production has been resumed in some of the mines, but enough remain abandoned to provide adventurous exploring.

Furze bushes surround Dunboy Castle, a nineteenth-century ruin of little interest to the art historian but set in a lovely landscape. Nearby pastures and hedges make excellent grazing for the horses of tinkers. Most of the wagons one sees are rented by vacationers, but sometimes a tinker will unexpectedly show up in one. Especially in the south, these descendants of the legendary Irish kings live by begging from tourists. They have little in common with the gypsies of the Continent, and they have preserved the fierce pride that is ascribed to the clever tinkers of the sagas, who were able to perform seemingly impossible tasks.

On the opposite shore of the bay lies Bantry House, a country estate. Though less tastefully furnished than Adare Manor, it has a park that resembles a botanical garden and a spectacular view of the bay.

The road to Cork runs directly eastward, and several side trips down secondary roads are recommended. The stone circle of

Drombeg (illus. 8, page 36) stands in the middle of hilly fields near Glandore. All of the stones are standing except for the westernmost block, which lies flat on the ground. Excavation unearthed the bones of a person buried here at the time this cultic site was constructed, between 150 B.C. and 120 A.D. Some 130 feet to the west, the remains of two huts and a cooking hearth give some idea of the primitive living conditions in the third century A.D. Water was collected in a hollowed stone; experiments have shown that water could be boiled by heating the stone and could be kept warm for a short time afterward.

A second detour leads from Inishannon to *Kinsale*, on the mouth of the Bandon, which was the scene of fierce battles in the seventeenth century when the Spanish sought to break the English rule in Ireland. Spanish troops under del Aguila were be-sieged by English soldiers until Ulster rebels came to their aid. But when the Spaniards and the Irish proved unable to agree on strategy, the English were easily able to destroy the Irish and drive the Spaniards from the country. Today, Kinsale is a crowded beach resort, and mackerel fishing, as along the entire south coast, is one of its main industries. Things to see in Kinsale include the pub The Spaniards, St. Multose Church, whose northwest tower from the early period of construction in the twelfth century rises—most uncommonly—above the transept, and French Prison Tower in Cork Street, from a much more recent era. Charles Fort, 2½ miles south of Kinsale, dates from the sixteenth century and resembles other castles of this period previously described. Its weakened masonry makes it extremely dangerous to enter.

A third side trip, this time to the north,

An 1856 steel engraving of Glengariff.

Some 19th-century views of Cork. TOP: *Sunday's well;* CENTER: *the Father Mathew statue;* BOTTOM: *the North Mall, from the River Lee above the North Bridge.*

brings one to the abbey of Kilcrea. Cormac Laidir MacCarthy had this cloister built some 500 years ago. Especially interesting are its sacristy and its writing room with countless windows.

Cork is a busy port city. With 130,000 inhabitants, whose low houses press tightly together along the banks of the Lee, it ranks as the island's third largest city, after Dublin and Belfast. The natives proudly proclaim that Cork will come to surpass Dublin in the future, and when one sees the number of oil tankers, refineries, and industrial plants around the harbor, this prediction seems quite plausible.

When St. Finbarr founded a monastery here in the sixth century, the settlement rapidly flourished, and with its cloister school it soon resembled a small city. Danish warriors conquered the district in the ninth century, and they in turn were driven out two centuries later by the next wave of immigrants, the Anglo-Normans. A number of uprisings began here, and as a result Cork soon came to be called "Rebel City." During the Irish Civil War, 1919–1921, the city was considerably ravaged.

The old Marsh section of town, between two arms of the River Lee, is an inviting place to stroll. St. Patrick's Bridge forms the center of the city; the present one with its three arches was built in the nineteenth century after a tidal wave destroyed its predecessor. The well-known Cork Public Museum stands in Fitzgerald Park and houses impressive historic and prehistoric collections. In Gillabbey Street, one ought to visit St. Finbarr's Cathedral, built in the neo-Gothic style in the eighteenth and nineteenth centuries on the site of a considerably older church.

In Father Mathew Street, where it meets Father Mathew Quay, stands the Father Mathew Memorial Church (also called Holy Trinity Church). This tireless campaigner for accommodation between the Catholic Irish and Protestant English also advocated a sharp decrease in the Irish consumption of alcohol. His statue stands on St. Patrick's Bridge.

Crossing the bridge to the other bank of the Lee, one soon comes to the emblem of Cork, St. Anne's Church, whose bells can be heard all over the city. Its oddly shaped tower, partly sandstone, partly limestone, is known locally as the "Pepper Pot Tower" because of its unusual point. Looking back at the opposite bank, one is struck by the Church of Christ the King, which was built thirty years ago and is one of the most modern churches in Ireland.

Before leaving the Cork area, one must not miss *Blarney Castle*, 5 miles to the northwest, a survivor from the fifteenth century in a lovely garden landscape. The

A 19th-century view of Blarney Castle.

249

Round tower of Cloyne.

castle has an L-shaped tower from the time of its builder, Cormac Laidir MacCarthy, and a chapel on the fifth story, but tourists descend on the spot for other reasons. Since the reign of Elizabeth I, people have come here to climb to the top of the tower, bend backward over the edge, and kiss the Blarney Stone, which is supposed to make one a good speaker. The attendant on duty to assist with this dangerous gymnastic exercise is bound to relate the story that Queen Elizabeth, after the local lord kept finding new ways to avoid surrendering his castle to the Crown, exclaimed that his excuses were "all Blarney . . . " To talk Blarney is to lie—but in a charming way.

By way of Midleton, one comes to the cathedral and nearly 100-foot round tower of *Cloyne*, built over 700 years ago; nothing has survived of the monastic settlement that stood here in the sixth century. The philosopher George Berkeley (author of *A Treatise Concerning the Principles of Human Knowledge*; died 1753) served as bishop of the present cathedral for eighteen years. The Cloyne portal is adorned with the St. Anthony's cross and the Egyptian tau cross, which suggest the influences of the cultures of the Mediterranean.

Youghal, a popular vacation spot and beach resort at the mouth of the Blackwater River, has often served as a military base for the Irish and the English during the course of its 700-year history. After the defeat of the rebellious earl of Desmond, the king rewarded one of his true vassals, Sir Walter Raleigh, with large tracts of land and the Tudor house called Myrthle Grove. Raleigh is said to have been the first to cultivate the potato in Ireland. This initially appeared to be a blessing for the country, but following the potato blight and poor harvests of the nineteenth century, it revealed itself as a curse. The introduction of tobacco is also credited to this nobleman. After Raleigh's execution, Youghal came into the hands of Richard Boyle, who fought off local rebels until Cromwell's troops took over this function and used the town as a base for raids into the interior.

In St. Mary's Church, from the early thirteenth century, one is struck by the indentations filled with clay plates that serve to improve the acoustics. Remarkable graves lie next to the tomb chapel of Richard Boyle and his wife.

Portions of the former fortifications have survived in the old part of town, and in the middle of the main street is the Clock Gate, fortified with two semicircular towers. Today, it houses a historical museum and the Tourist Office, which always seems eager to assist the traveler. Across from Youghal stretches the coastal county of Waterford.

Graves in St. Mary's Church, Youghal.

Waterford

Ardmore—Helvick Head—Waterford

The Blackwater and the Suir in the east border this hilly landscape that gently slopes to the sea. Its coastline is broken by the bays of Dungarvan, Tramore, and Waterford.

The monastery ruins and round tower dominate the hillside of *Ardmore* and provide a panoramic view over the broad sweep of Ardmore Bay. St. Declan, the founder of the monastery, was bishop of Munster when St. Patrick began his work. This fact is one of the few definite proofs that there were Christians in southern Ireland before the coming of the great proselytizer. Ardmore belonged to the estate of Sir Walter Raleigh, and it was later devastated by Cromwell's troops.

In the tall, slender, well-proportioned round tower from the second half of the twelfth century, which is perhaps the loveliest one in Ireland, one can detect a slight, and quite uncommon, entasis—a subtle swelling toward the center and corresponding narrowing toward the top. The tower is separated into five stories connected by ladders, each marked by a circular band of stones. The top story has four windows opening toward the main directions of the compass, and it supports a typical conical roof.

Moelettrium O Duibh-ratha commissioned the cathedral of Ardmore before 1203 and had it embellished with details seldom encountered elsewhere. The beautiful west window and the blind arcades on the interior walls of the church are especially strik-

Figures from the west wall of Ardmore Cathedral.

ing. The exterior gable ends have rows of arcades on top of each other with extraordinary reliefs that resemble those on some of the high crosses. The archangel Michael and other "Continental" saints who appear here were seldom portrayed in Ireland; Adam and Eve, the three kings, and the Judgment of Solomon, though, are familiar from the Bible crosses. During renovation of the nearby oratory, ascribed to St. Declan, two stone blocks with Ogham inscriptions were discovered behind the gable.

Ardmore's peaceful setting encourages long walks along the raw cliffs, the last one will encounter on this journey. The spot seems to be ideal for a longer stay, but one ought to allow two days to see Tipperary and return to the ferry landing. Directly to the north, via Linsmore, whose cathedral was renovated by Richard Boyle in about 1635—and where one can see the tomb of the MacGrath family, from 1557, with relief depictions of a crucifixion, St. Patrick, St. Gregor, St. Katharine, and various apostles —one can take a side trip to the great St. Mellery Monastery in the foothills of the Knockmealdown Mountains.

It is quicker, however, to proceed northeastward by taking the road to Dungarvan, a small industrial town. Before Dungarvan, at Ringville, one can turn off to the popular scenic viewpoint at *Helvick Head*. From here, one can look out across the broad bay and its flat shores as well as back toward the mountain chains of the interior. At the beach resort of Tramore, one turns northward to *Waterford*, a harbor city of 30,000 inhabitants on the south bank of the Suir. After joining the River Nore where three counties, Waterford, Wexford, and Kilkenny, meet, the Suir forms the elongated bay of Waterford Harbour. Southwest of Waterford, at Knockeen, there are several dolmens that warrant a brief stop, though they do not

"St. Declan's Head," the remains of a tomb in a corner of Ardmore Cathedral.

equal the one at Browne's Hill in size.

The original structures of Waterford have almost totally disappeared, but quite a number of medieval buildings have survived. The city was loyal to the king, and its coat of arms displayed the motto *Urbs intacta manet Waterfordia*. Its first settlers were Danes under the leadership of Sitric, who founded a small defensive settlement here in about 850. Reginald Tower, the fortified tower on the river, got its name from the Danish governor Reginald MacIvor in 1003. In the eleventh century, Danes and Irish fought side by side here against the new invaders, the Normans under Strongbow, who were ultimately victorious. This tower, nearly 1,000 years old, has since served as a lookout tower and prison. Today, it houses a museum in which a number of treasures are preserved, notably ornamental swords and countless autographs of English monarchs. Prince John, who became king in 1199, gave a particularly beautiful ornamental sword to the town of Waterford and also determined its boundaries. Shortly afterward, Richard II enacted a Charter Roll (almost any medieval royal legal document was called a "Roll"), which would be followed by twenty more. Elizabeth I granted autonomous status to Waterford, but the most important document here is the charter of Charles I from 1626. This not only confirmed all the rights of the city, but also accorded it the right to distill whiskey, "uisce beatha," whose Gaelic name literally means "water of life."

Not far from Reginald Tower stands the French Church, a former convent from roughly 1240. The east window of its chancel is especially beautiful. In times of war, this church has served the citizens of Waterford as a hospital.

Lastly, one must not neglect the popular glassware that makes Waterford famous. On tours through the factory, one can watch the glassblowers at work.

Tipperary

Ormond Castle—Clonmel—Cahir Castle—Tipperary—Athassel—Cashel—Holycross Abbey—Roscrea—Kilcooly Abbey—Ahenny

This landlocked county, whose name is famous thanks to the English soldiers' song, can be toured in various directions. Either one can turn back into the interior just before the end of the trip, or one can include the most important segment of the county in a tour of Leinster—following the River Suir to Tipperary, turning off toward Cashel, and returning via Thurless to Kilkenny.

St. Mary's Church, Clonmel.

Similarly, a visit to the northern portion of Tipperary can easily be combined with a tour of the Shannon Plain and Lough Derg; it can be approached from either Killaloe or Portumna.

Tipperary extends from the Suir Valley to the Shannon Plain and comprises two old regions known as the South and North ridings. This is the grain-producing section of Ireland, hilly and thickly settled, and steep ranges of limestone mountains run through it.

At the actual mouth of the Suir, which lies far inland, sits Carrick-on-Suir. Here, *Ormond Castle*, the palace of the Butlers, the dukes of Ormond, stands in the middle of a lovely park (illus. 74, page 178). This Elizabethan structure was enlarged for the queen herself in 1568. It is embellished with plaster medallions of animals from the Ormond coat of arms in the west wing and plaster portraits of Elizabeth I and Thomas, earl of Ormond, in the portal. A restored portion of the mansion gives some idea of its appearance at the time of Elizabeth. (Those who will not be returning to the vicinity of Carrick-on-Suir should now drive to Ahenny and its crosses, described at the end of this section.)

Following the Suir, one soon comes to *Clonmel*. On the east edge of this village it is

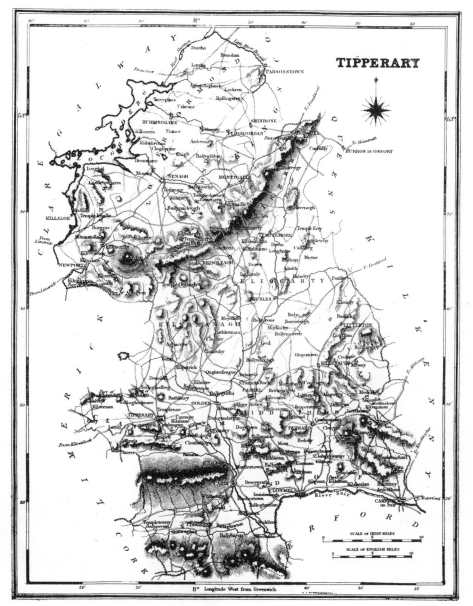

Map of Tipperary from Samuel Lewis's atlas, 1837.

255

possible to visit a falconry, and in the village itself stands St. Mary's Church, which was begun in the thirteenth century. The greater part of the structure, however, including the east and west windows, dates from the fifteenth century.

Just beyond Clonmel, the Suir turns southward, only to describe a large curve past Ardfinnian before rejoining the main road at Cahir. *Cahir Castle* towers over all of the other buildings in this town. It was built by Conor O'Brien (1142) and rebuilt by the Butlers, and it was long held to be invincible. But after a ten-day siege in 1599, the Earl of Essex succeeded in conquering it. After having been destroyed by Cromwell, the castle was once again rebuilt. Thanks to the conscientious work done at that time, it is quite well preserved. Circular and polygonal towers strengthen its massive outer walls; a three-story crenelated tower stands in the center of the space within. None of the original interiors of Cahir Castle survive, but the structure alone provides a vivid picture of English might. In Cahir there are a number of good hotels.

One proceeds northwest via Bansha to *Tipperary*. Because this town occupies a somewhat elevated spot, it can be seen from a great distance away, and the approach to it thus seems endless to the hiker—as it did to infantrymen in the past.

Tipperary enjoys a contemplative calm, and the pleasant conversation in its local pubs, which are busy even in the morning,

Cahir Castle.
RIGHT: *Cahir Castle, from the southeast.*

seems to exemplify Irishness. The town is also well known as a center of horse breeding, and cattle markets are frequent here.

Athassel, reached by the straight road to Cashel, is consecrated to St. Edmund. A small bridge leads to the twelfth-century abbey, which was built for the Augustinians by someone named de Burgo. The abbots of Athassel had great secular influence as peers of parliament until the area fell to the Ormonds. The church has a central tower and another tower on the northwest side. A roughly 600-year-old tomb with representations of Norman knights has been fitted into the south wall.

A drive of only a few minutes brings one of the highlights of the journey into view,

Entrance to Athassel Abbey.

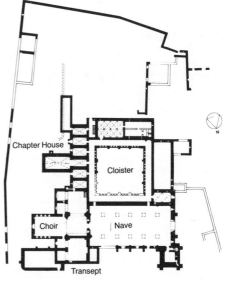

Ground plan of Athassel Abbey.

RIGHT: a 19th-century view of the Rock of Cashel; BELOW: ground plan of the Cashel Cathedral.

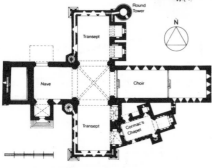

Cashel (illus. 86, page 185). Seen from a considerable distance, this huge granite dome was the site of an early Celtic royal seat. In the Middle Ages, Cashel was the stronghold of the southern Irish clergy. Even from afar, one can distinguish the contours of individual buildings on "Caiseal Mumhan" ("the stone castle of Munster").

Cashel probably began in the pre-Christian era as a Celtic settlement. Beginning in 370 A.D., with Eoghanachta, it became the seat of the kings of Munster and remained so for the next 700 years. When St. Patrick reached the castle in the course of his mission, King Aenghus was on the throne, and he willingly converted to Christianity. At the king's baptism, the saint is said to have inadvertently jabbed his staff into the king's foot; the monarch, thinking this a part of the ritual, endured it stoically. Cashel soon became a bishopric, and it was not uncommon for the king himself to fill that high spiritual office. Cormac MacCuilleannain (the first Cormac), a gifted poet and the builder of the round tower on the Rock, was one of those who served both functions. He died in 908 at a battle near Ballaghmoon, during an attempt to become high king. In about 977, Brian Ború had himself crowned in the church at Cashel, and about a hundred years after Cormac had fallen, he too died, at the Battle of Clontarf. Another hundred years were to pass before Muircheatach O'Brien finally presented the Rock of Cashel to the church, whereupon building of a new church, still partially preserved, was begun.

Under Bishop Cormac MacCarthy (the second Cormac), in the incredibly short space of seven years between 1127 and 1134, Cormac's Chapel (illus. 87, page 186) was built. This treasure of Irish architecture and stonemasonry was consecrated in the presence of all the dignitaries in Ireland. Cashel then soon became the archbishopric, and in 1169, Domhnall Mor O'Brien began the construction of a cathedral, of which portions from the thirteenth century remain. During the reign of Henry VII, Gerald FitzGerald, an enemy of the archbishop, burned the bishop's palace to the ground. He justified his deed to the English king with the explanation that he had thought the archbishop to be in residence. In spite of the protests of the Catholic church fathers, Henry VII named FitzGerald, the "Great Earl," as his viceroy; his authority virtually amounted to that of an independent sovereign.

One notable prince of the church was Miler MacGrath, a Catholic bishop who converted to Protestantism, an act that was rewarded by Elizabeth I when she named him an Anglican bishop as well. He was, for some years, a bishop of both faiths, and he held other high offices also. When Miler MacGrath died at the age of one hundred, it was reckoned that he had served in some seventy official capacities.

Behind the Hall of the Vicar's Choral, there is a cross with relief depictions of St. Patrick and a crucifixion; the usual animals and ribbon ornaments of the early period of high crosses embellish its base. Its badly weathered foundation stone is traditionally

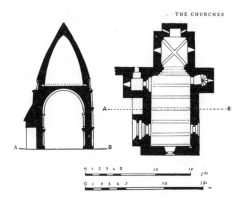

Section and ground plan of Cormac's Chapel.

held to have previously been a coronation stone (like Lia Fail, Tara, and Meath).

Cormac's Chapel represents a turning point in Irish art. Its use of new architectural elements testifies to the adoption of Continental styles. The Roman church and the various monastic orders brought their own concepts here, and these were soon combined with traditional Gaelic forms to create the Irish Romanesque style.

At the time of its construction, Cormac's Chapel was assuredly one of the largest projects in Ireland, and it rapidly influenced the design of other churches. Cormac recruited not only stonecutters from Ireland but also noted artists from the Continent, and the stone carving here once more shows how easily the Irish could blend foreign artistic styles with their own sense of form. The blind arcades, the cross-ribbed vaulting, and the tympanum in the north portal of the carefully restored church are strongly marked by Continental influences. The delicate ornamentation of the doorway, the capitals, and the columns, however, reflect the individual artistic experiences of the native stonecutters. On the tympanum, a centaur armed with a bow and arrow is hunting a lion. The columns are adorned with human faces of various kinds and intricate designs.

Two square towers flank the steep roof, which is fully preserved. The roof itself appears to be patterned after those of the earliest wooden churches and oratories. A group of figures arranged in a curve around the chancel exhibit Mongol features, in part, and some of them wear Egyptian head coverings. Blind arcades along all the walls cause the space to appear larger than it is. A sarcophagus on the west side reveals Scandinavian influences and still bears traces of earlier painting. In fact, it is assumed that the entire interior of the chapel was once brightly painted.

The magnificent thirteenth-century cathedral is a model of Gothic architecture (illus. 86, page 185). Through the years, the lancet windows, the lovely rosette in the gable wall, the side aisles, and the broad central tower were added to the original choir. In accordance with the English custom, there are a number of tombs in the nave, and Bishop Miler MacGrath lies in the south transept. The absence of a roof by no means lessens one's impression of a timeless dignity.

During its long period of prominence, Cashel survived repeated attacks and fires, but in the eighteenth century it began to fall into ruin. The visitor should allot a generous amount of time to see the castle's many artistic and historical features (open 10:00 A.M.–8:30 P.M. in summer; to 7:00 P.M. in winter). The best view of the hill of Cashel is to be had from the north or from the ruins of nearby Hore Abbey, a Benedictine house.

North of Cashel, right on the road leading toward Thurles, lies *Holycross Abbey*. The abbey takes its name from a relic of the True Cross that the pope presented to the

king of Munster in 1100. It is now preserved by Ursuline sisters at Cork. In front of the entrance to the church, there is a stone block with a Romanesque depiction of the Crucifixion. The church and the monastery buildings have been superbly restored in recent years. Missing portions of the roof have been replaced and the sculptures have been cleaned, so now one can discover

carvings of human figures and animals, including a charming owl, on the buttresses below the cross-ribbed vaulting.

The chancel is one of the masterpieces of fifteenth-century church architecture, and the nave with its ornamented arches is roofed with Gothic ribbed vaults. The roof is more recent and has been carefully renovated, as have portions of the cloisters. In the north aisle is one of the few examples of Irish fresco painting. Using only brown, red, and green, three figures, a tree, and a hart are disposed in a hunting scene of delightful simplicity. Two of the hunters armed with bows follow a third who carries a hunting horn and a dog on a leash. The hart stands behind the overly stylized tree. Thanks to the Butlers of Ormond, Holycross Abbey

Holycross Abbey.

Funeral procession depicted on the base of the North Cross, Ahenny.

survived for a hundred years after the secularization by Henry VIII. Scarcely anything remains of the monastery buildings.

At Holycross, Tipperary's North Riding begins. Here, there are only a few artistic monuments of interest. One quickly comes to the Shannon Plain by way of Thurles, and one can view what is left of Nenagh Castle, which was burned by Irish rebels in 1548. Near the northern boundary of the county, at Portumna, are the ruins of the thirteenth-century church of Lorrha as well. Both Nenagh and Lorrha can easily be included in the Shannon tour, or if one is pressed for time, they may be omitted. By continuing southeast—or north if one approaches from Thurles—one soon comes to *Roscrea*. Roscrea Castle, built by King John in 1213, is less interesting than the twelfth-century St. Cronan's Church, of which only the façade survived destruction in the eighteenth century. Its Romanesque main doorway with round arches is topped by a triangular gable in which the large figure of a bishop is carved. It is said to represent the sixth-century founder of the church, St. Cronan. Smaller, unornamented blind arches flank the main portal.

Across the street are the remains of a round tower, and north of the church there is a late high cross with the figure of Christ and a bishop (possibly St. Cronan). On the shaft of this cross, there are not only male figures but female ones as well, which is most unusual in Irish art.

Via Thurles one re-enters the South Riding. *Kilcooly Abbey* lies in the middle of a ducal estate. One enters it through a small passageway next to the main gate. This Cistercian abbey, north of the Slieveardagh Hills, should by no means be missed. In about 1200, several monks came from nearby Jerpoint Abbey in order to consecrate this church, built by Donal Mor O'Brien, to the Holy Virgin. Years later, when this church was destroyed, a much larger structure was begun in roughly 1445. In its chancel there are stone seats for the abbot and his assistants, and the figures of St. Christopher and St. Bernard stand against the walls. Next to the Butler coat of arms there is a stone mermaid coyly playing with her mirror and surrounded by fish.

One main attraction of the abbey is the grave of the abbot Philip (died 1463), who played a large role in the construction of the new church. Another is the tomb of Piers Fitz Oge Butler (died 1526) in the choir. It was executed by the sculptor Rory O'Tunney, who signed it, "Roricus O Tuyne scripsit." Ten dignified figures in long robes carry the sarcophagus with a recumbent knight on top. Each of these saints and church fathers is holding a symbolic object in his hand; books, axes, chalices, and crooks are the external signs of these scholarly bearers.

Following secondary roads, one now drives southward through the Slieveardagh Hills to reach Slievenamon, on the east side of which the high crosses of *Ahenny* stand in the middle of a small cemetery. A sign on route L26 points across a small bridge and past a few houses to a slope that the road begins to climb. Some 325 feet beyond the houses, a smaller sign points down the hill, and here one must climb over the wall and walk down to the cemetery.

These two early crosses (illus. 33–35, pages 46 and 47) of the Slieveardagh group (eighth century), to which the crosses, at Kilkieran in Kilkenny also belong, are the only remains of what was once a monastic settlement. On the base of the North Cross, there are priests with croziers and a funeral procession in which a beheaded figure is being carried on horseback. At the front of this procession, a man is carrying a wooden cross that closely resembles surviving stone ones. On each of the Ahenny high crosses, all of the figural ornaments are restricted to the base, which is more than 3 feet per side. Their slender shafts are reserved for ornamental compartments with various Celtic ribbon symbols. Some of these interwoven designs precisely correspond with patterns in the Book of Kells. Where the cross ring intersects with the cross itself, there are intricately ornamented bosses derived from goldsmithing. Atypical "hats" top these crosses, which are probably the oldest true high crosses in Ireland.

From Ahenny it is not a very long drive to the coast. Jerpoint Abbey lies along the route again, and once more one passes through the exquisite garden landscape of Wexford, with its meadows and pastures in infinite variations of green. The sparkling water of Rosslare Harbour is green, too, creating a colorful backdrop for the white ferry.

PRACTICAL TRAVEL SUGGESTIONS

THE IMAGE OF THE IRISH

This green island on Europe's western edge demands openness and receptivity from its visitors, for they are constantly presented with new and unexpected images and impressions. It is easy to meet the people, for the Irish not only love to talk but are also accepting and curious about all things foreign. It is difficult to characterize the Irish in brief; the national character encompasses the most contradictory elements: generosity and helpfulness, boundless passion and temper, unconcern for the future, even a distant fatalism, along with intense political views.

Irish storytellers have a flair for words. Because of the country's long suppression and isolation, these talents, which elsewhere threaten to disappear in this technological age, are highly developed here. And Ireland's folk music is as impressive as its literary and narrative arts. Sadly, there are few *shanachies*, or professional storytellers, left, but folklorists have managed to preserve much of the stock of traditional sagas in the past century. The foreign visitor is struck by Ireland's Gaelic heritage and its natural blend of the new and the traditional.

Agricultural workers and small farmers compose much of the population. In the last 150 years, roughly 4 million Irish have emigrated; the high birth rate, though, has kept the population stable. An unbroken cultural tradition, a strong religiosity, and traces of superstition stamp the lives of the rural populace, though the government has been only mildly successful in its attempts to revive the Gaelic language and customs. The country dwellers' pleasures are simple: frequent visits to the cinema and many social gatherings, at which there is a wealth of banter and singing. Irish urban life is, except in certain details, fully comparable to city life in Britain or on the Continent.

It would be a good idea, for at least part of your trip, to avoid the characterless, modern luxury hotels that have sprung up in the last few years and stay at a "bed and breakfast" house. Here, you should have an opportunity for interesting conversation, and your hosts will doubtless offer some good sightseeing suggestions.

For a comprehensive tour of Ireland, you should allow about three weeks (excluding transit time there and back). Those with less time to spend should limit themselves to only a part of the country. No one season is to be especially recommended; with luck, one can eat breakfast outside in February or November. May, June, or September might be preferable, not only because of the weather but also because of the calm and solitude that simply don't exist during the peak months of July and August.

TRAVEL

Two organizations will be very helpful to the tourist planning a vacation in Ireland. The C.I.E. (*Córas Iompair Éireann*), or the National Transport Organization, runs public transportation in Ireland and is also the country's largest travel bureau. The B.F.E. (*Bord Fáilte Éireann*), or the Irish Tourist Board, will provide much valuable free information. Both have branches in New York City.

Air connections

The national airline, Aer Lingus, flies to the United States and nearly every other country in Europe. The main airports are Collinsbridge (Dublin) and Shannon (Limerick). Flights within the country are inexpensive and connect Dublin with Belfast, Cork, and Shannon. Regular flights to the Aran Islands are offered by Aer Arann, 62 Dominick Street, Galway. Telephone (091) 6-51-10 or 6-51-19.

Ferry connections

There are many ferries that travel between Britain and Ireland. One of the most popular runs between Fishguard (Wales) and Rosslare (Wexford). Other ferries travel between Swansea and Cork, Holyhead and Dun Laoghaire (Dublin), Liverpool and Dublin, Preston and Belfast, Preston and Larne (Northern Ireland), Liverpool and Belfast, Ardrossan and Belfast, and Glasgow and Belfast. These crossings take between three and twelve hours. The price of transport-ing an automobile is calculated according to the length of the vehicle (this is explained thoroughly in the ferry timetables). A brochure issued by the Tourist Board, "Car Ferries to Great Britain and Ireland," provides up-to-date information.

There are also several direct ferry connections to Ireland from the Continent (Rotterdam–Dublin, Le Havre–Rosslare, and Cherbourg–Rosslare). These voyages take about twenty-one hours each.

During the main tourist season, it is advisable to reserve space on the ferry through a travel agent.

Trains and buses

Traveling in Ireland without a car is difficult but not impossible. Trains and buses go to even the smallest villages, but the journey will take considerably longer than it will by car. Both trains and buses are operated by the National Transport Organization (C.I.E.). They are not necessarily the best means of transportation, but they are reliable. The prices are reasonable and there are many reduced fares, including those for students.

Vacationers in the Republic of Ireland can use trains and buses as much as they wish with a Rambler ticket (*except* within the cities of Dublin, Cork, Limerick, and Galway). Rambler tickets are available at all C.I.E. offices and at all major train stations in Ireland. You will have several options when purchasing a Rambler ticket. You may buy a ticket valid on trains *and* buses, or one valid on trains *or* buses; tickets are good for eight or fifteen days. Children under sixteen travel for half-fare.

Overlander tickets resemble Rambler tickets, but they are also valid in Northern Ireland. The Overlander is a fifteen-day train *and* bus ticket.

In Northern Ireland, there are especially economical summer tickets, valid for seven days. Children under fifteen pay half-fare.

Traveling by car

Even though there are no freeways, the roads are well constructed, and even the smallest country lanes are paved, though often a bit narrow. There is so little traffic that driving is a pleasure, and driving on the left soon becomes a habit. There are a few necessary restrictions that must absolutely be observed. The speed limit is generally 55 mph, 30 mph in towns. To drive in Ireland, you must have had a valid U.S. driver's license for at least two years. Car telephones and CB radios may be taken into the country but not used.

Cautions: Right-hand right of way applies in Ireland, despite the fact that cars are driven on the left. A double white line at the side of the road means that parking is prohibited.

In Ireland, seat belts are required, and children under twelve must ride in the back seat of a vehicle. Motorcyclists must wear helmets. Visitors to Ireland are *not* exempt from these regulations. Handicapped persons with permits may park free at any parking meter in Ireland.

Patience is needed when driving in rural Ireland, not because of the traffic (which is moderate) but because of the many donkeys, cows, and sheep that are pastured but not fenced in. Livestock are likely to cross the roads, and they must be given the right of way. Traffic in the towns is moderate; Dublin traffic can be fairly heavy.

Since no spot on the island is more than 60 miles from the coast, it does not take long to get anywhere.

Numerous shipping companies are available to serve those who wish to bring their own cars; these firms' brochures are updated annually and are available through travel agencies.

Renting a car

Rental cars are readily available everywhere; they are inexpensive in the off season and cost about as much as they do in other countries during peak season. The rates are based on the usual daily or weekly rental plus a mileage surcharge.

Important: Depending on the firm, the minimum age for drivers runs from twenty-one to twenty-five. If you plan to cross the border into Northern Ireland with a rented car, you must advise the rental agency of your intention beforehand. Motorcycles and mopeds are *not* available for rent.

Many travel organizations offer flight-and-rental-car arrangements (with or without hotel reservations). These all-inclusive arrangements provide unlimited mileage at no extra charge.

WHAT TO TAKE

Rainwear and sweaters are musts due to the swift changes in weather. Anyone who intends to be outside a great deal (and is prepared to take the weather in stride) will above all need sturdy shoes—boots would even be better—for walking through swampy ground or wet fens. Light hiking shoes would be good to have in any case.

Rain in Ireland seems to come from all sides, so an umbrella is almost useless. An anorak, a parka, or a light raincoat should provide better protection. Some kind of headgear is advisable because of the wind.

RECREATION AND SPORTS

This book is mainly intended for travelers who are interested in art and are open to new impressions. It is a guide to a unique cultural landscape, assisting the reader to structure an individualized stay somewhat off the beaten track. But anglers and golfers will also find Ireland ideal. And even the most determined sightseer can easily fit in a break for swimming and sports.

Swimming

Swimming is possible nearly everywhere, even in Donegal, though those who are accustomed to Florida, California, or Mediterranean waters will not be terribly comfortable. Water temperatures of around 14–16° C (57–61° F) are closer to those of resorts on the North Sea or in Maine. Swimming off flat beaches is generally quite safe, but it is important to be aware of the changing tides. It is always wise to ask the residents about local conditions.

Boating

In most areas, it is inexpensive to rent a motorboat by the day. However, the more than 550 diesel-driven cabin cruisers that ply the Shannon and the canals have become more expensive in recent years due to increasingly heavy demand. Anyone can operate one of these 20- to 40-foot boats on the Shannon or on the lakes without prior experience. It is necessary to reserve early, however. A guidebook containing precise navigational maps, information about fuel stations, shopping, and places to buy water is provided when the boat is picked up; the most important operating tricks and regulations are also explained. For safety, these boats are not rented to anyone traveling alone, and operators must be at least twenty-one years old. Generally, a deposit is required, refundable when the boat is returned. Diesel fuel is not included in the rates; maintenance costs must also be assumed by the person renting the boat. The largest boat marina is at Carrick-on-Shannon. There are packages available that include flights, transfers to Carrick-on-Shannon, and boat rental.

Important:

- Always keep to the right, especially on narrow curves in the river.
- Always pass black signs (buoys, beacons, or poles) on the left.
- Because of the shallows and numerous islands, especially in the lakes, keep to the marked channels.
- Before entering Lough Ree and Lough Derg, you must be absolutely certain to inquire about weather conditions; these waters can be extremely dangerous in a storm.
- Never attempt to land where there is a soft bottom; there is a danger of clogging the intake vents that cool the motor.
- It is illegal to operate a boat after dusk.

The Shannon has six locks; the Grand Canal, forty-four. From April 1 to September 1, the Shannon locks are generally open from 9:00 A.M. to 6:00 P.M. In other months, the hours of operation are considerably more limited.

The Shannon is not navigable below Killaloe. On the Shannon, it is possible to fish from one's boat for pike, perch, salmon, and trout. A license for a week is very inexpensive and is available in every village.

Boat tours

Boat tours are available on loughs Gill, Corrib, Key, Derg, and Ree and on the Barrow, Nore, and Suir rivers. The Galley restaurant-ships travel regularly between New Ross and Waterford.

Other possibilities (all reasonably priced) include:

Aran Islands
Blasket Islands (Ring of Kerry)
Dalkey Island (near Dublin)
Ireland's Eye (north of Dublin)
Tory Island (Donegal)
Skellig Rocks (Ring of Kerry)
Inchbofin (Connemara)
Garinish Island (West Cork)
Saltee Island (Wexford)

Camping

There are a great many campgrounds in the vicinity of Dublin, but they are also easy to find elsewhere. If there is no campground nearby, you might ask the local landowners for permission to camp.

Campsites may be rented at reasonable prices by the night or by the week. In Northern Ireland camping is more expensive. To rent camping equipment, contact O'Meara Camping Ltd., Main Office, Sunshine Works, 160A Crumlin Road, Dublin 12. Telephone: (01) 75-23-14.

Hang gliding

March to October are the best months for hang gliding. Every hang glider must have adequate liability insurance, available through a one-month guest membership in the Irish Hang Gliding Association.

Before making a start hang gliding in Ireland, it is necessary to contact the Irish Hang Gliding Association, Randal Gillham, Secretary, 31 Clonard Drive, Dondrum, Dublin 14. Telephone: (01) 98-05-58. The association has three affiliate clubs: the Cork Hang Gliding Club; the Waterford Hang Gliding Club, and the Connaught Hang Gliding Club, Foxwood, County Mayo.

Beginners may attend short courses through most clubs or at the Airsport Hang-Gliding School in Glenageary, County Dublin.

Gliders and equipment may be rented (check with the Association). The best hang gliding areas are:

Knockalla, Donegal
The Great Sugarloaf, Wicklow
Lacken Bowl, Wicklow
Mount Leinster, Carlow
Musheramore, Cork
Mweelin, Cork
Portmagee, Kerry
Dingle Peninsula, Kerry
Arra Mountains, Tipperary
The Devil's Bit, Tipperary
Maamturk Mountains, Galway
Minaun Heights, Achill Island
Ox Mountains, Mayo
Slieve Anieran, Leitrim
Ben Bulbein, Truskmore, Sligo

Cycling

Bicycles may be rented in many places. Rental costs include insurance; tandems and saddlebags are also available. In case of minor breakdown (flat tires, for example), you are expected to make or arrange for repairs yourself. When traveling longer distances, you can break up the trip by carrying the bicycle on a train or bus for a stretch, if space is available. You will be charged an additional one-fourth of the normal one-way fare.

After prior arrangement with the renter, it is possible to drop off the bicycle at another location, though a surcharge will be imposed.

Fishing

Information bulletins and brochures available from the Tourist Office outline where fishing is free and where there is a fee. You do not need a state license to fish fresh-water fish, except for salmon. You will also need a state license, available from local tackle dealers, to fish the heavy runs of sea trout. Irish fishers are almost exclusively interested in salmon and trout. Therefore, the waters where these fish are found are more expensive and more crowded.

The season for fishing salmon is spring; for all other fish, June–September. Several kinds of license are available, all reasonably priced. There are licenses valid for an entire season in one district only or in all districts. Temporary licenses are available for seven days or for twenty days and are good in all districts. The owners of fishing waters (whether individuals or associations) have the right to charge special fees. Most of the larger hotels own their own fishing grounds; these are available for use by the guests of the hotel.

The fish are generally relatively large and are known to be good fighters, so strong poles and lines and large lures are recommended. It is best to buy spinners on the spot.

Fishing with live bait is generally prohibited. It is also illegal to use more than two poles in the water at the same time. The best fishing area is Lakeland, the Irish lake basin, where one lake runs into another and many are connected by rivers or canals. Between spring and fall, the Lakeland fishing competitions are held here. The flat country of County Clare covers a smaller area, but it is just as attractive to fishermen as that of Lakeland.

The western (Atlantic) coast offers excellent opportunities for deep-sea fishing. Boats designed for the high seas go out in search of halibut, rays, shark, perch, and mackerel. Lobster, crab, and mussels are plentiful. Complete fishing holidays are available, including air transportation and hotel; often, even license fees and boats are included in the package.

At the best spots, there are paths and parking spots. Boats are also available, some with outboard motors. If you wish, you can hire a fishing guide.

Apart from salmon and trout, the most important fish are:

Pike: year-round, in the large lakes from March to November; record—about 41 lbs.

Bream: best time, May–October; record—about 12 lbs.

Tench: best time, June–October; record—about 7½ lbs.

Rudd: best time, June–October; record—about 2¾ lbs.

Roach: best time, June–October; record—about 2¾ lbs.

Perch: year-round; record—about 5½ lbs.

Carp: record—about 18¾ lbs.

Eel: year-round; record—about 6 lbs.

Flying

Three international airports (Dublin, Cork, Shannon), about twenty smaller airstrips, twenty-two Irish aero clubs, and four gliding clubs offer their services to visitors interested in flying. For further information, contact the Aircraft Owners and Pilots Association, PO Box 927, Nassau Street, Dublin 2. Telephone: (01) 77-25-62.

Golf

In Ireland there are sixty-eight 18-hole golf courses and well over a hundred 9-hole courses. Equipment can be rented in most places, and beginners are permitted on the greens immediately.

Sports unique to Ireland

Various types of sport quite popular in Ireland are virtually unknown to Americans.

Hurling is a lawn game similar to hockey, with teams of fifteen players.

Gaelic football is a special kind of football in which the players may use their hands but neither pass the ball nor run with it.

Greyhound racing is nearly as popular as horse racing. There are races almost daily, generally in the evening, at twenty tracks throughout the country. For further information, contact *Bord na gCon* (Irish Greyhound Racing Board), Henry Street, Limerick. Telephone: (061) 4-67-88.

Hunting

Fox hunts are very popular in Ireland. During the season, from November 1 to the end of March, there are hunts almost daily. Hunting societies are delighted to welcome guests who are excellent riders.

There is a participation fee (cap fee) per hunt, and you will be able to rent a mount. It is possible to book an all-inclusive tour.

Small-game hunting on horseback is especially popular and widespread. The main season is in November. In the western part of the country, battues are held between September and January.

The hunting of snipe and wild ducks is quite popular and rigidly controlled. Pheasant cock hunting was recently legalized. Grouse and partridge may be hunted, but certain birds—pheasant hens, quail, and brant geese—are rigidly protected. Hunting is totally forbidden in many nature conservation areas, and tourists may not hunt deer.

The hunting seasons (usually from September 1 to January 1) are established each year by the Irish Ministry of Agriculture. Rabbits and foxes may be hunted year-round.

Anyone bringing a weapon into Ireland is required to have a weapons certificate from the Irish Ministry of Justice (Secretary of the Department of Justice, Upper Merrion Street, Dublin 2). This is a formality for hunting weapons and can generally be taken care of through a travel agency.

Ornithology

Of 380 varieties of birds to be seen in Ireland, 135 nest there. Many of them migrate south in autumn. Migratory birds (snow geese) come from Iceland and Greenland to spend the winter in Ireland. In the lake areas there are colonies of wild swans, wild geese, ducks, wading birds, sea swallows, and sea gulls.

In meadows and forests one sees blackbirds, song thrushes, goldcrests, chaffinches, bullfinches, and siskins. The moors and marshy regions are inhabited by curlews, snipes, skylarks, dickeybirds, sea gulls, and wild geese.

Along the Atlantic coast, with its wealth of fish, you will find falcons and sea gulls; wild ducks at the broad mouths of the rivers;

oystercatchers, whistling ducks, wild geese, and swans. On the south and west coasts, storm petrels and gannets build their nests.

For more detailed information, contact the Irish Wildbird Conservancy, Southview, Church Road, Greystones, County Wicklow. Telephone: (01) 87-57-59.

Horses, riding, and horse-drawn carriages

About sixty riding clubs and hotels throughout Ireland keep horses available for hire. Details can be obtained from the Irish Tourist Board.

The normal Irish breed, the hunter, is a horse of many uses. The capabilities of this half- to three-quarter-blood animal range from normal riding to fox hunting and jumping. The ponies are well known for their obedience, endurance, and good temper.

Riding schools offer beginning classes, classes in jumping and dressage for advanced riders, and above all lovely rides. A certain amount of experience is necessary for the pony treks, which generally last a week and on which one is required to sit in the saddle for about four hours a day (baggage is transported from one stop to the next). The most interesting treks are in Connemara, on the Dingle Peninsula, and in Sligo.

Addresses and information about riding holidays are provided in the brochure "Horse Riding Holidays." All-inclusive arrangements usually combine air transport, hotel, and four hours' riding daily. For further information, contact *Bord na gCapall* (Irish Horse Board), St. Maelruan's, Tallaght, County Dublin. Telephone: (01) 51-05-22.

For those interested in polo, there are training courses available that require considerable riding ability. Information is available from Whitfield Court Polo School, Waterford. Telephone: (051) 8-42-16.

The Royal Dublin Society Horse Show takes place annually during the first full week of August and attracts horse lovers and trainers from all over the world. Dressage trials and races are included in the program. The winners and many foals change hands here, often for exorbitant prices. Nearly half of all show jumpers get their horses from Irish stud farms.

Horse-drawn carriages for leisurely travel may be rented by the week. This is a slow means of transportation, so you should not expect to travel as far as by car. Gypsy wagons are usually furnished with four beds and bedding, built-in cupboards, and propane stoves. They are not geared toward the luxury-oriented. These are especially common in the south, around Cork; they can cover up to 12½ miles a day. A list of farms where they may be parked is provided with the rental. You should avoid the main roads with a horse and wagon, but there are plenty of smaller, well-paved roads to choose from. Three people or more can rent an extra riding horse for their wagon for a surcharge. When picking up a wagon, a deposit is commonly required. Here, too, inexpensive, all-inclusive arrangements are available.

Caution: There are special traffic signs that indicate whether horse-drawn carriages ought to avoid a stretch of road (if there is too steep a climb, for instance).

Canoe trips and fast-water running

These activities are possible in many areas. The best rivers are the Liffey, Barrow, Nore, Boyne, Slaney, Lee, Shannon, Suir, and Munster Blackwater.

Favored lake regions are Dublin Bay, Portnoo and Rossnowlagh (Donegal), Archill Island (Mayo), Glenbeigh (Kerry), and Tramore (Waterford). For further information, contact the Irish Canoe Union, Mr. Stephen Stronach, Development Officer, Room 9-10, 4-5 Eustace Street, Dublin 2. Telephone: (01) 80-98-39. Fifty local clubs are federated in this organization.

Sailing

This sport has a long tradition in Ireland. The Royal Cork Yacht Club, founded in 1720, is the oldest sailing society in the world.

Sailing schools on the Irish Sea, the Atlantic, and the inland lakes offer beginning courses and rental boats.

Diving

The Irish coastal waters offer visibility up to 100 feet and contain a variety of fauna and flora. The Gulf Stream has a favorable influence on the water temperature, which averages 17° C (63° F) down to 65 feet, 14° C (57° F) between 65 and 100 feet, and 10° C (50° F) below 100 feet.

A number of diving schools offer their services, especially during the best diving season, April–September. For further information, contact Mr. John Geraghty, Honorary Secretary, Irish Underwater Council, 60 Lower Baggot Street, Dublin 2. Telephone: (01) 78-78-44.

Tennis

Tennis is very popular. A number of hotels have tennis courts, and the fees are modest. Lawn courts are used almost exclusively. For more information, contact C. J. Brennen, Honorary Secretary, Irish Lawn Tennis Association, 15 Cill Eanna, Rahenny, Dublin 5. Telephone: (01) 33-89-16.

Hiking and mountain climbing

With its broad beaches and gentle hills, Ireland is an inviting place to hike. Informa-

tion about the 300 forest parks in Ireland is given in the brochure "The Open Forest," available from the Tourist Board. Anyone interested in botany will be especially intrigued by the vegetation in the southwest. With very few exceptions, this guide gives no tips on hiking, for quite good and precise information is available locally. At the local tourist offices, one can get small brochures about hiking trails in the vicinity. Those planning to hike more extensively in a given area may wish to buy the "Ordnance Survey Map" of that district, available in bookshops.

Most of the forest parks have marked hiking trails, nature paths, and picnic grounds. They are under the supervision of the Forest and Wildlife Service, 22 Upper Merrion Street, Dublin 2. Telephone: (01) 78-92-11.

Climbing at all levels of difficulty is possible in Ireland. Difficult granite walls and defiles in the mountains and splendid cliffs along the coast offer interesting challenges for even the jaded climber.

The best areas are:

Wicklow: Glendalough, Luggala

Dublin: Dalkey Quarry (practice cliffs), the cliffs of Bray Head and Ireland's Eye (except during bird-nesting time)

Donegal: Derryveagh Mountains, Lough Barra, the cliffs of Malinbeg, near Glencolumbkille

Clare: limestone cliffs near Doolin

Galway: Ben Corr in the Twelve Bens, Maamtrasna, and Colum Gowaun (sandstone)

Kerry: Sneem, Brandon, Cloon Lake near Glencar, and the Gap of Dunloe

Water-skiing

Excellent opportunities for this sport are offered on the flatter ocean shores; lakes and rivers are also used. Equipment can be rented. For more information, contact Mr. Alan Dagg, Irish Water Ski Association, 43 Finsbury Park, Dublin 14. Telephone: (01) 95-11-41.

Surfing and wind-surfing

Beautiful surf is to be found at a number of spots along the coast. Here are a few of the best areas:

East coast: Bray, Brittas Bay, Magheramore, Jack's Hole, and Courtown. Surf higher than 3 feet only when there is a strong wind.

South coast: Tramore Beach, Annestown, Bunmahon Bay, Garrettstown, Courtmacsherry, Barley Cove, Inchadoney, Owna-hincha. Surf from 3 to 8 feet year-round.

Southwest coast: Derrynane, Waterville Bay, Reenroe Beach, St. Finan's Bay, Inch, Slea Head, Brandon Bay, Ballyheigue, Banna Beach, and Ballybuinion. Surf from 3 to 11 feet year-round.

West coast: Doughmore, Spanish Point, Silver Beach, Lahinch, Cornish Point, Moy Bay (Creg), and Fanore Beach. Surf from 3 to 13 feet year-round.

Northwest coast: Achill Island (Dooagh, Keel Beach, Minaun Cliffs, Dooega), Enniscrone, Easkey, Aughris Quay, Strandhill, Bundoran, Tullan Beach, Rossnowlagh, Glen Bay, Glencolumbkille, Loughros Beg Bay, Rosbeg, Marble Beach, and Rosapenna. Surf from 3 to 13 feet year-round.

EATING AND DRINKING

Irish meals are generally simple. There is much lore and countless sayings about food ("An egg without salt is like a kiss from a beardless man"), but a culinary tradition similar to that of France never developed. All is not potatoes and porridge, however. Ireland is well known for its excellent beef, and its shellfish is plentiful and delicious.

Irish specialties include smoked salmon, prawns, oysters, lobster, grilled trout, Limerick ham, and mushrooms. In addition to these dishes, the major hotels offer international—mainly American—cuisine.

Seek out the good (but sometimes expensive) hotel restaurants that offer Irish specialties. Dinner is served very early, between 6:30 P.M. and 9:00 P.M. Later than this, it is impossible to get anything to eat in the hotel restaurants.

The Chinese restaurants offer another possibility. In addition to Chinese dishes, they also offer European fare. These restaurants are often open later, usually until as late as 11:00 P.M. In this way, you can stay on the road somewhat longer and make use of the evening sunlight.

There are regional differences in Irish cuisine, and it is possible to find dishes prepared with considerable flair. It is also interesting to note that, according to UN statistics, the basic Irish diet is one of the most nutritious in the world.

Breakfast cannot be had before 8:30 A.M. at the earliest, for the Irish are late risers. "The hours between 7:00 and 10:00 are the only ones in which the Irish tend to be monosyllabic," wrote Heinrich Böll in his *Irish Journal.* Anyone wishing to start out earlier will likely have to do so on an empty stomach. But breakfast is worth the wait, because here it is the foundation for the entire day and is even larger than its English counterpart. Tea and coffee are everywhere. Porridge is being replaced by corn flakes, which are served as a first course, before rashers and eggs and sausages. (Note that in Ireland, *bacon* denotes pork fat for cooking; the breakfast meat is known as *rashers*.) Occasionally, you will also be served kippers. Along with the above, toast, soda bread, or homemade brown bread is served; English bread is also available. There is never a shortage of excellent salted butter and jam.

Lunch is eaten between 12:30 P.M. and 3:00 P.M.; in contrast to the English custom, it is the main meal of the day. A basic lunch might consist of potatoes with various meats (including mutton), followed by a dessert. The potatoes are boiled, seldom fried. Only in the fish-and-chips shops can one get French fries (or the Irish version thereof). The various kinds of steak are famous, as are the diverse ways of preparing fish. Vegetables are served simply, often enhanced by neither spices nor sauces, so the fare may seem somewhat monotonous to the visitor looking for exotic fare. Irish butter (salted) is an important export item and of the highest quality. Cheese is produced, but there is no truly unique Irish type. Desserts are rich, in the English tradition.

Afternoon tea is as much a part of the daily ritual as it is in England and is served between 4:00 P.M. and 6:00 P.M. Dinner has gained in importance over the last few years. In place of these two meals, many of the hotels serve a *high tea*, at which wine or tea and meat or fish sandwiches are served. Again, there is much butter and the famous soda bread.

Bars and restaurants

In the Irish bar, which resembles the Eng-

lish pub, there is rarely anything more than sandwiches to eat. If you wish a more complete meal, go to a hotel restaurant.

Bar hours: Weekdays from 10:30 A.M. to 11:30 P.M., Sundays 12:30 to 2:00 P.M. and 4:00 to 10:00 P.M. In Dublin and some of the towns, bars close from 2:30 to 3:30 P.M. Closing time from October to May is 11:00 P.M. Closing time is marked by the singing of the Irish national anthem.

Hotel restaurants are much patronized by the Irish themselves. More and more specialty restaurants are springing up, and over the past few years French cuisine has ceased to be an unknown quantity. American-style snack bars are also making their appearance, especially in Dublin.

Each year, the Irish Tourist Board issues the extremely helpful brochure "Dining in Ireland," which is organized by county and village and lists all the recommended eating places and their hours, specialties, and prices.

Beverages

Irish hospitality focuses especially on drinks, of which several truly deserve their excellent reputation.

Tea, which is usually served quite strong, is first-rate and is consumed at all hours of the day and night. In fact, the Irish have the highest per capita tea consumption in the world. Most drink it black, many use milk and sugar, but virtually no one uses lemon. Coffee lovers will be bitterly disappointed. There is only one solution: drink tea.

Good and famous beers have been brewed here for centuries (including stout, ale, and lager), of which Guinness tops the list and accounts for the highest export figures (especially to England). The distinctive Guinness flavor is said to come from the water of the Liffey. One orders beer by the bottle or the pint. Dark beer is favored by the Irish.

Whiskey—produced from barley, with or without the addition of malt—is another national drink. It differs from the Scottish variety mainly due to a different manner of distilling; also, Irish whiskey is produced only in Ireland, whereas Scotch is made all over the world. About five major brands are available, and most are produced in the Republic. *Potheen*, the illegally distilled whiskey, is aged for a shorter amount of time. It is sharper in taste than whiskey and generally of inferior quality.

IRELAND FROM A TO Z

Accidents

The emergency number to call everywhere is 999. All accidents in which personal injury is involved must be reported to the police. After exchanging personal data with the other parties involved, immediately notify your insurance agents. For assistance, contact the Irish Visiting Motorists Bureau, 5-9 South Frederick Street, Dublin 2. Telephone: (01) 77-45-69 or 71-94-43.

Further help may be obtained from the branches of the Automobile Association (AA):

Cork, 9 Bridge Street—(021) 50-51-55
Dublin, 23 Suffolk Street—(01) 77-94-81
Dundalk, Market Square—(042) 3-29-55
Galway, Headford Road—(091) 6-44-38
Limerick, Arthurs Quay—(061) 4-82-41
Portlaoise, Fintan Lalor Avenue—(0502) 2-16-92
Sligo, Wine Street Car Park—(071) 50-65
Waterford, Meaghers Quay—(051) 7-37-65

Accommodations

Accommodations are relatively inexpensive. A room (with a generous breakfast) in a private house is the least expensive. Bed and breakfast in a guesthouse is moderately priced; hotels cost somewhat more, especially the luxury hotels. In all price ranges, there is a wide selection and rooms are easy to find, especially off season.

The Irish Tourist Board publishes several brochures annually. "Irish Homes" (listing private residences and farmhouses) and "Hotels and Guesthouses" provide precise information about rates and facilities.

Automotive repairs

Repairs are available for all makes. Mechanics for rare makes are only found in Dublin. Hours: Monday–Friday, 9:00 A.M. to 6:00 P.M.

Banks

Banks are open from 10:00 A.M. to 12:30 P.M. and 1:30 P.M. to 3:00 P.M.; on Thursdays in Dublin, banks are open until 5:00 P.M.

Books and travel literature

There are many bookshops in Dublin with a large selection of Irish and English literature. Maps are also sold, as are special titles dealing with Gaelic language and history.

Children

The Irish are very fond of children. One

should encounter no problem taking children and teenagers along.

Climate

The Irish climate is more moderate than England's and is milder than that of other countries on the same latitude because of the Gulf Stream. The record temperatures are -17° C (1° F) and 32° C (90° F). The average temperature in summer is 15° C (59° F). In winter, the temperature seldom falls below freezing; in summer, it rarely climbs above 25° C (77° F). Precipitation varies between 28 and 100 inches a year; snow is rare. The sunniest months are May, June, and September (with an average of five to six hours of sun a day), but even in these months, damp, cool weather may predominate. Brief, generally warm showers and rapid changes in the weather are typical of Ireland.

Constitution

The constitution of the Republic (1937) refers to the entire territory of the island, but six counties of Ulster are still part of the United Kingdom. Ireland is an independent republic ruled by a parliament. The parliament consists of a house of representatives and a senate. A president, elected directly by the people, serves as head of state for a seven-year term. A prime minister heads the government. The constitution declares that Gaelic is the official language of the country. Gaelic is a required course in the schools, and the mastery of this language is a prerequisite for holding any public office. In actual fact, the second official language, English, strongly predominates.

Cost of living

It is impossible to generalize, for prices in the countryside differ greatly from those in the city. Statistics show that, in terms of prices, Dublin falls right behind New York and ahead of most European capitals.

Crafts

In some parts of the country, there are vacation courses in glassblowing, weaving, pottery, and basketweaving. For information, write to The Administrator, I.C.A., An Grianan, Termonfeckin, County Louth, *or* The Executive Officer, Crafts Council of Ireland, Thomas Prior House, Ballsbridge, Dublin 4.

Currency and foreign exchange

The Irish pound is the national unit of currency. A pound consists of 100 pence. Ireland now belongs to the European Monetary System and has its own exchange rate independent of the British pound. (The American equivalent is about $1.15.)

Having been detached from the British pound, the Irish pound has become cheaper. It is advantageous to purchase most of your Irish pounds at home and exchange only supplementary amounts in Ireland itself.

Caution: Your bank may need time to order sufficient Irish banknotes.

Travelers cheques and Eurochecks are accepted at all banks, but not necessarily by all hotels and businesses.

There is no restriction on the amount of money you may bring into the country—except for gold coin. However, you may take *out* only £100, or £250 in foreign currency, more than you brought in.

Dogs and other pets

Pets should not be brought along, for they are subject to a quarantine of at least six months.

Roughly eighty packs of hounds are maintained in Ireland. Of these, only two are trained for deer hunting, but there are a number of packs available for fox hunting in every county. Greyhound racing is a favorite sport. One famous racing hound, Master McGrath, has even had a monument built to him.

Economy

The industrialization of the country is steadily progressing. Though the Irish recognize its importance, they characteristically harbor numerous reservations about it. Ireland's entry into the Common Market was a question of survival. Today, the country is chiefly occupied with fighting unemployment. Agriculture is still the most significant segment of the economy and employs the most people. Tourism, horse breeding, brewing, and whiskey production are other major sources of income. The country has very few mineral resources. A state organization supervises the retrieval of fuel from the peat bogs.

Electrical current

220 volt, alternating current. Adapters for wall outlets are available in all electrical shops.

Farmhouse holidays

These are ever more popular, for you can drive through Ireland in your own car or in a rented one and have a whole chain of farmhouse accommodations to choose from.

The Irish Farm Holidays Association publishes a catalogue, more than 100 pages long, with photos of all the farmhouses in the organization. This simplifies the search for these accommodations, which often resemble manor houses, by the way, rather than farmhouses. The catalogue also indicates which houses have tennis courts, fishing grounds, or riding horses available. During the main tourist season, it is advisable to make a reservation the day before you plan to arrive. These houses feature a cozy, family atmosphere; guests are usually introduced to one another.

Folklore

The Irish Folklore Union coordinates the activities of the local societies around the country and can provide information about the roughly thirty folklore festivals held annually. Write to Comhaltas Ceoltoiri Eireann, Culturlann na hEireann, Belgrave Square, Monkstown, County Dublin.

Geography and related statistics

Ireland lies between 51°30′ and 55°30′ north latitude and 5°30′ and 10°30′ west longitude.

Length from north to south: 364 miles
Width from west to east: 170 miles
Overall area: 32,589 square miles
Republic of Ireland: 27,106 square miles; 2.9 million inhabitants
Northern Ireland: 5,483 square miles; 1.5 million inhabitants

The population is, on the average, relatively old. Because of emigration, the percentage of fifteen- to thirty-four-year-olds is very small. The population density of Northern Ireland is more than twice that of the Republic.

Ireland is divided into thirty-two counties; twenty-six of these belong to the Republic of Ireland, six to Northern Ireland. These counties make up four historical provinces: twelve belong to the eastern province, Leinster; six to the southern province, Munster;

five to the western province, Connacht; and nine (including the six in Northern Ireland) to the northern province, Ulster.

Only three cities (Dublin, Cork, Limerick) have populations of 50,000 or more; all the remaining towns have 30,000 or fewer inhabitants.

There are large areas of heath, peat bog, and moor, with more than 100 inland lakes. Pasture land composes 50 percent of the total area; cultivated land, 20 percent, and forest, only 3 percent.

More than 2 million tourists visit Ireland each year.

Greetings

Especially in the countryside, you are almost always expected to exchange a friendly greeting. These greetings differ somewhat from those in England, however. "Good afternoon" is almost never used; instead you will hear, even shortly after noon, "good evening." "Good night" is not only used on parting in the evening but also as a common greeting. Yet the Irish are not terribly fussy—someone might just say "hello."

Hitchhiking

This is a common practice in Ireland. Irish drivers are happy to pick up travelers standing beside the road, and tourists may safely follow their example.

Houses for rent

The Irish Tourist Board publishes a listing of houses for rent. The minimum rental period is one week.

Import and export duties

The following goods may *not* be imported: weapons, munitions, and fireworks of any kind; birth-control devices; exotic birds; rabbits and other carriers of bacteria; hay and straw and anything that has been packed with them; monkeys and animals susceptible to rabies; pornography; narcotics; and fruits, meat, animal products, fowl, and all foodstuffs. Dogs and cats (except those coming from Northern Ireland or the Isle of Man) require a six-month quarantine.

The following goods are *subject to duty* on entering Ireland: clothing; porcelain; clocks of all kinds; sweets; coffee; glassware; jewelry; leather goods; automobiles and motorcycles (except those to be used personally by tourists); musical instruments; recordings and record players; radios; wines, spirits, and tobacco of all kinds (excepting duty-free quantities); and toys.

For more specific information, consult the Collector of Customs and Excise, The Custom House, Dublin, *or* The Secretary of the Revenue Commissioners, Dublin Castle, Dublin.

The following may be taken out of the country *duty-free*: the usual duty-free goods (1 liter of spirits, up to 250 grams of tobacco, 200 cigarettes, and so on), perfumes, and other items declared as gifts up to a value of $400.

It is best to inquire about the precise regulations on the ferries and at the airports.

Information

Information desks at the Irish Tourist Board are open Monday through Friday, from 9:00 A.M. to 6:00 P.M.; Saturday, from 9:00 A.M. to 1:00 P.M. Service is excellent.

Sources of information outside Ireland are: Irish Tourist Board, 590 Fifth Avenue, New York, New York 10017; CIE Tours International, 590 Fifth Avenue, New York, New York 10017; and Irish House, 150 Bond Street, London W.1.

Languages

Despite efforts to keep it alive by concerned organizations, Irish Gaelic is dying out. No more than 30,000 Irish now speak Gaelic as their first tongue; the remainder can only remember studying it in school. Even though Gaelic is the official language of the country, English strongly predominates. Even with the *Gaeltacht* (the Gaelic-speaking Irish), one can get along quite well with English. Any foreigner who can speak even a few words of Gaelic is considered a marvel; however, he or she may not be understood because there are as many dialects of Gaelic as there are clans. A Gaelic speaker from Cork will have trouble understanding one from Waterford or Donegal.

English is perfectly adequate for travel purposes. Should you wish to learn Gaelic, however, summer courses are given by the Institute of Irish Studies, 6 Holyrood Park, Dublin 4. Telephone: (01) 69-24-91.

Medicines and pharmacies

Since pharmacies are few and far between, it is best to bring your own medications and over-the-counter drugs in sufficient supply. Birth-control pills are available in limited selection in Dublin, but not in the interior. Importing medicines is forbidden; one is permitted only enough for personal use during his or her stay.

Pharmacies are open weekdays from 9:00 or 9:30 A.M. until 6:00 or 7:00 P.M.; Sundays from 11:00 A.M. to 1:00 P.M.

Personal documents

For vacationers (staying up to 3 months), a valid passport is sufficient (no visa is needed). Citizens of the United Kingdom do not need a passport.

Postal service and telephones

In smaller villages, post offices are usually part of a general store. Post offices are open from 9:00 A.M. to 6:00 P.M. Many smaller rural ones are closed for lunch. Postal and telephone fees are high.

Coin-operated telephones are a little different from those in America and may addle a tourist unused to them. Here are a couple of points to remember:

• When the desired party answers, press the button marked "A."
• Collect calls can only be handled by the long-distance office (dial 10).
• Calls to the emergency number (999) are free.

Real estate

Interested parties may obtain information from Irish Auctioneers and Estate Agents, 38 Merrion Square, Dublin 2. Telephone: (01) 76-20-11 or 76-34-51.

Religion

Ninety-five percent of the population of the Republic is Catholic, and, though not always obvious, the church is still one of the strongest forces in the country. There are also smaller Protestant and Jewish congregations. Sunday masses are crowded, and the churches are well attended even on weekdays. After 200 years of suppression, the Catholic faith was able to flourish again after 1829.

In Northern Ireland, only 35 percent of the population is Catholic. Here, the majority is Protestant; the largest denominations are the Anglicans (Church of Ireland) and the Presbyterians.

Service stations

Ireland has a good network of service

stations, so you can find gasoline even in remote areas. Gas pumps are usually in front of the general store in the smaller villages, and various familiar brands are available. For safety reasons, it is illegal to carry spare canisters of fuel.

Service stations are open nearly everywhere from 8:00 A.M. to 6:00 P.M., though not all of them are open on Sunday.

There are three types of gas:
Top grade (super)—98/99 octane
Middle grade (mix)—95/96 octane
Lower grade (regular)—about 90 octane

Shopping and souvenirs

Tweed garments, from ties to suits, can be tailor-made and shipped home quite inexpensively. Woolens, such as ties and the popular hand-knitted cardigans and pullovers, are cheapest in rural areas (Donegal and the Aran Islands). Leather goods are not cheap but are top quality.

Shopping hours are generally from 9:00 A.M. to 5:30 P.M. There are no fixed hours in rural areas, but since the shop and the owner's home are usually in the same building, it is often possible to shop until late at night.

Ireland has not been spared the flood of tawdry souvenirs, but a few items are worth recommending. The small St. Brigid's crosses, for instance, woven of straw and traditionally given on the saint's day, are tasteful remembrances.

Small pieces of jewelry are made out of Connemara marble (a green stone that is not truly marble), and Waterford crystal, of course, is much in demand and highly prized. In addition to tweed clothing, one can also find tweed dolls and bookmarks with Gaelic ornamentation. Exquisite porcelains are made in Belleek (Fermanagh). At Newgrange, you will find candles with archaic symbols on them as well as expensive gold bracelets patterned after historic pieces. There are also small reliefs made of pressed peat in the form of crosses—miniature replicas of the high crosses.

Record shops offer a vast quantity of Irish music, unfortunately often of poor quality. But well worth recommending are recordings by Sean O'Riada, who strives to present Irish folk music in authentic fashion, and by the Flingels and the Dubliners, who represent a more modern trend. From marches and harp music to classical music, everything is available. Most recordings display a seal on the wrapper that reads "guaranteed unplayed."

Foreign tourists may shop inexpensively and avoid paying purchase taxes in Northern Ireland by showing their passports.

Students

The Students' Travel Bureau, 5 St. Stephans Green, Dublin 2, provides all kinds of information, operates vacation camps, and helps students find inexpensive accommodations.

Taxis

Taxis are available in all towns and are generally less expensive than their counterparts in the United States or Britain. There is a minimum fare for the journey, and there are surcharges for additional passengers, additional luggage, and trips on holidays or after midnight.

Time

Greenwich Mean Time applies in Ireland; between about March 23 and October 26, Daylight Saving Time is in effect.

Tipping

The standard rates should be given in bars and restaurants, and taxi drivers and hotel personnel expect about 10 percent. One also tips hairdressers and doormen. Porters expect a small tip per bag. In restaurants, a service surcharge of 10 to 12 percent is automatically added onto the check.

Tourist Offices

Nearly every town and village has one. Here are some of the most important:
Cork, Monument Buildings, Grand Parade
Dublin, 14 Upper O'Connell Street; 51 Dawson Street
Dun Laoghaire, Moran Park
Galway, Aran Fáilte, Ireland West House
Limerick, 62 O'Connell Street
Mullingar, Delvin Road
Sligo, Stephen Street
Waterford, 41 The Quai
Youghal, Clock Gate, Main Street

The Tourist Office in Dublin publishes a weekly calendar of events that provides a free listing of plays, movies, bars, and restaurants.

Traffic signs and directions

Traffic signs are so similar to the international standard that no special instructions are needed here. Speed limits are given in miles. Sign posts give names in English and Gaelic. Special green signs point to places of interest.

When receiving directions, be aware that your informant may be thinking in old Irish miles, which are nearly twice as long as regular ones. When Great Britain introduced the metric system, Ireland went along. The change is only taking place slowly, however, so that both systems are in use today.

Youth exchange

The following language schools provide information on *au pair* vacations in Ireland:
Dublin School of English, 11 Westmoreland Street, Dublin 2. Telephone: (01) 77-33-22 or 77-32-21.
The Language Centre of Ireland, 9 Grafton Street, Dublin 2. Telephone: (01) 71-62-66.

Youth hostels

The Irish Youth Hostel Association (ANO-IGE) maintains fifty hostels around the country. Almost all of them are open year-round. There is no age limit for pass holders, but no one may stay more than three consecutive nights in any given hostel. Youth hostel passes are required and may be obtained from the Irish Youth Hostel Association, 39 Mountjoy Square, Dublin. Telephone: (01) 74-57-34.

NOTES

NOTES

NOTES

NOTES

N O T E S

CHRONOLOGY

c. 6000 B.C.	The island is settled by Mesolithic fishermen and hunters.
c. 3000 B.C.	Beginning of a second wave of immigration, marked by felling of the forests and construction of the first megalithic graves.
beginning in 500 B.C.	Gaelic-speaking tribes take possession of the island and erect primitive settlements and ring forts. The Druids practice their cult ceremonies, perhaps in stone circles although these were already ancient. Small clans (*tuatha*), with a warlike ruling class, appear. High Kings, together with their troops, the *fianna*, become the subjects of countless sagas.
c. 200 A.D.	Appearance of the Ogham alphabet. Celtic ornamentation on enamel and gold objects is of high quality.
c. 250	Cormac MacArt attempts to unify the clans from Tara. The chief of his *fianna* is the legendary Fionn mac Cumhail (Finn MacCool).
c. 450	Raiders bring to Ireland a British youth, Patrick; the boy flees to France, where he is trained in theology, then returns to Ireland as a bishop. According to legend, St. Patrick lights Easter fires at Tara as a symbol of the conversion of Ireland. At about this time, the Uí Néill ("sons of Niall," or O'Neills) become Ireland's most powerful and most famous royal dynasty.
5th–9th centuries	Irish monasteries develop and come to exercise great influence on the intellectual life of Europe. Churches are built of wood and later of stone. The first illuminated manuscripts are created.
c. 800	The first ornamental crosses develop out of earlier stone forms. The art of illumination enjoys its culmination. Vikings occupy portions of the country and plunder the monasteries.
841	Danes found a settlement that will develop into Dublin, as well as other villages along the coast.
1014	High King Brian Ború defeats the Vikings, but falls in the Battle of Clontarf. High crosses are now richly decorated with depictions of Bible stories. Round towers are built to protect the monasteries.
1022	End of the dominion of Tara; decline begins.
1110	Ireland finally is subjected to the Roman clergy. Dioceses are set up and the monastic orders extend their power.
1134	Cormac's Chapel is dedicated in Cashel.
1169	Diarmuid MacMurchada, an ousted king, summons the Normans under Richard de Clare (called Strongbow), the Earl of Pembroke, into the country. Norman nobles take possession of three-fourths of the land. The first monasteries of the Continental monastic orders are founded; late figured crosses date from this period.

1210	The first survey of counties.
1318	The Irish offer the crown to Edward Bruce, brother of Robert Bruce, the Scottish king. After Edward's defeat at Faughart, independence is lost for six centuries.
1394	Richard II occupies the country and orders massive fortresses built.
1494	All of the independent barons are required to subject themselves to the English crown (Henry VII).
c. 1535	Henry VIII secularizes nearly all of the monasteries after having broken with the Pope over his divorce. Soon afterward, Henry VIII declares himself King of Ireland. Ireland continues to be Catholic.
1579–1603	Desmonds, FitzGeralds, O'Neills, and O'Donnels lead a rebellion lasting a number of years, which is decided at the Battle of Kinsale in 1601 with the defeat of the Irish. Munster is devastated. The English counts build elaborate manor-houses in the English style.
1608	England colonizes the North with Protestant settlers.
1641	Rebellion against the Protestants in Ulster.
1649–50	Cromwell's troops devastate the countryside.
1688	The exiled James II lands in Ireland, is supported by the populace, but defeated by William III (of Orange).
1690	The soldiers who fought for James II flee by the thousands to the Continent and are employed as mercenaries in the armies of Austria, Russia, Italy, etc.
1691	New rebellions take place on account of the rigid suppression of Catholicism.
1777	Formation of the first major resistance movement, "The Volunteers." Demand for an independent parliament.
1782	England recognizes the new Irish Parliament and its legislation fully, but the government is made up solely of Protestants.
1798	A new rebellion, this time supported by France, fails.
1800	The "Act of Union" makes Ireland part of England. Several rebellions follow.
1829	Daniel O'Connell demands the political emancipation of the Catholics.
1847	The high point of the Great Famine, which was brought about by potato blight and poor harvests. Mass emigration results. The population falls from 8 to 4 million.
1858	The emigrants found a secret society, the Fenians, with the goal of liberating Ireland.
1893	Founding of the Gaelic League.
1905	Founding of Sinn Féin.
1916	The Easter Rebellion. The Republic is declared. The rebellion is defeated by the English after four days.

1919–21	War of independence against England.
1921	The Treaty of Inverness. Ireland is recognized as a free state within the Commonwealth. The desire for full sovereignty leads to civil war.
1932	The Republicans come to power under the leadership of Eamon de Valera.
1937	Referendum and a new constitution.
1939–45	Ireland remains neutral in the Second World War.
1948	A coalition government under J. A. Costello fixes the name of the country as the Republic of Ireland. England declares Ireland no longer a member of the Commonwealth.
1965	The Prime Ministers of the two parts of the country meet and agree to work closely together.
1969	Northern Ireland becomes the scene of countless bombings, battles, and reciprocal acts of terrorism by the IRA and URA.
1973	Ireland enters the European Common Market together with England. De Valera announces his retirement.
1975	De Valera dies.

BIBLIOGRAPHY

Landscape, Art, Culture

Barrow, George Lennox, *The Round Towers of Ireland*. Dublin, 1979.

Brandt-Förster, Bettina, *Das irische Hochkreuz*. Stuttgart, 1978.

Bryant, Beth, *Ireland on 15 Dollars a Day*. New York, 1980.

Burl, Aubrey, *Rings of Stone: The Prehistoric Stone Circles of Britain and Ireland*. London, 1979.

De Breffny, Brian, *Castles of Ireland*. London, 1977.

————, *The Churches and Abbeys of Ireland*. London, 1976.

Gorman, Michael, *Ireland by the Irish*. London, 1963.

Harbison, Peter, *The Archaeology of Ireland*. London, 1976.

————, *Guide to the National Monuments of Ireland*. Dublin and London, 1970.

Henry, Françoise, *Croix Sculptées Irlandaises*. Dublin, 1964.

————, *Irish Art in the Early Christian Period*. London, 1965.

Irish Verse. London, 1970.

Kunz, Hans, *Irland, Grünes Vorland im Atlantik*. Walter, Olten and Freiburg,1971.

Leask, Harold G., *Irish Castles and Castellated Houses*. Dundalk, 1977.

MacLiammoir, Michael, *Irland*. Zurich, 1966.

MacLoughlin, Adrian, *Guide to Historic Dublin*. Dublin, 1979.

Merian: Irland, Vol. 29, No. 5. Hamburg.

Morton, Henry Vollam, *Irlandreise*. Frankfurt, 1978.

Norman, E. R. and St. Joseph, J. K. S., *The Early Development of Irish Society*. Cambridge, 1969.

O'Faolain, Sean, *The Irish*. London, 1947.

O'Riordain, Sean, *Tara*. Dundalk, 1971.

O'Sullivan, Donal, *Irish Folk Music, Song and Dance*. Cork, 1952.

Paor, Maire and Liam de, *Old Ireland*. London, 1958.

Pfister, Kurt, *Irische Buchmalerei*. Potsdam, 1927.

Sharkey, John, *Celtic Mysteries*. New York, 1975.

Treasures of Irish Art, 1500 BC–1500 AD. New York, 1977.

Wagner, Margit, *Irland*. Munich, 1968.

Wilson, David M., *Kulturen im Norden, Die Welt der Germanen, Kelten und Slaven 400–1100 n. Chr*. Munich, 1980.

Fairy Tales and Sagas

Carney, James, *Early Irish Poetry*. Cork, 1965.

Grimm, Brüder, *Irische Elfenmärchen*. Frankfurt, 1826.

Hetmann, Frederik, *Weißes Pferd, schwarzer Berg, Kindergeschichten aus Irland*. Weinheim, 1975.

MacManus, Seumas, *Die Königin der Kesselflicker*. Freiburg, 1965.

Müller-Lisowski, Käte, *Irische Volksmärchen*. Düsseldorf, 1962.

Lady Wilde, *Ancient Legends, Mystic Charms and Superstitions of Ireland*. London, 1888 (Reprinted: Galway, 1971).

ILLUSTRATION CREDITS

Black-and-white photographs

Henning Christoph, Essen, 6, 15, 16, 60, 71
Wolfgang Fritz, Cologne, 61, 62, 106
Michael George, 75
Karl Hublow, 9–11, 13, 14, 17, 19, 28–32, 34–36, 39, 45, 46, 50, 54, 55, 57, 94–97
Irish Central Tourist Office, Frankfurt a/M, 2, 5, 7, 8, 18, 24, 26, 27, 33, 37, 38, 48, 56, 66, 67, 70, 73, 76, 80, 82, 83, 114, 120, 124–127, 129–131
Foto Löbl-Schreyer, Bad Tölz, 41, 58, 72, 78, 81, 92, 93, 99, 108, 116–119, 122, 123, 128
Werner Neumeister, Munich, 1, 42, 43, 47, 49, 51, 52, 69, 79, 85, 86, 100–105, 110, 121
Maire and Liam de Paor, 20–23, 25
Kathy Ryan, 68, 88
Edwin Smith, 63, 89, 90, 107, 109, 113, 115
Wolfgang Ziegler, Vienna, 3, 4, 12, 40, 44, 59, 64, 65, 74, 77, 84, 87, 91, 98, 111, 112

Drawings and plans

Commissioners of Public Works, Dublin, fig. p. 163.
E. Maurice Craig, *The Architecture of Ireland*, London, 1982, figs. pp. 92, 199
Peter Harbinson, *Guide to the National Monuments in the Republic of Ireland*, Dublin, 1970, figs. pp. 25 (left), 26 (left), 30–31, 90, 98, 136, 170, 204, 218, 221
Françoise Henry, *Croix Sculptées Irlandaises*, Dublin, 1964, fig. p. 262
Françoise Henry, *Irish Art in the Early Christian Period*, London, 1965, figs. pp. 16 (left and top), 26 (center and right)
Françoise Henry, *Irish Art in the Romanesque Period*, Ithaca, 1970, figs. pp. 32, 130 (top), 132 (top), 209, 215, 259
P. W. Joyce, *A Social History of Ancient Ireland*, II, New York, 1968, figs. pp. 12, 13, 15, 17, 18, 23, 25 (right), 52, 58, 60, 93, 133, 141, 143, 169, 219, 246, 256 (left)
L. Russel Muirhead, *Ireland* (The Blue Guides), London, 1962, figs. pp. 105, 108
Sean P. O'Riordain, *Tara, The Monument of the Hill*, Dundalk, 1971, fig. p. 144
Liam de Paor, *Early Christian Ireland*, London, 1960, figs. pp. 130 (right), 131, 132 (bottom)
Maire and Liam de Paor, *Alt-Irland*, Cologne, 1960, figs. pp. 16 (bottom right), 19, 22, 24, 49, 96 (top), 129, 167, 171, 213
R. A. Stalley, *Architecture and Sculpture in Ireland, 1150–1350*, New York, 1971, figs. pp. 139, 163 (bottom), 257 (bottom right), 258 (bottom)
James Stevens, *Irish Fairy Tales*, New York, 1920, figs. pp. 63, 84.

INDEX

The text was set in ITC Garamond by U.S. Lithograph Inc.
New York.
The book was printed and bound by Novograph, s.a.
Madrid.